A CENTURY OF WOMEN

A CENTURY OF WOMEN

—❧—

Introduction by Jane Fonda

Edited by Alan Covey
Based on a documentary script by Jacoba Atlas
with Heidi Schulman and Kyra Thompson

Foreword by Pat Mitchell and Diana Meehan

TBS Books
Atlanta

Published by TBS Books,

an imprint of Turner Publishing, Inc.

A Subsidiary of Turner Broadcasting System, Inc.

1050 Techwood Drive, NW

Atlanta, Georgia 30318

"Thursday" and excerpt from Sonnet XI © 1922, 1950 by Edna St. Vincent Millay.
Excerpt from Sonnet XLII © 1923, 1951 by Edna St. Vincent Millay and
Norma Millay Ellis. From *Collected Poems*, HarperCollins.
Reprinted by permission of Elizabeth Barnett, literary executor.

"Cannery," © 1993 Carmen Tafolla.

Quotations pages 200, 203 from *Georgia O'Keeffe,* by Roxanna Robinson.
Reprinted with permission of HarperCollins.

First Edition   10 9 8 7 6 5 4 3 2 1

ISBN 1-57036-142-8

Packaged by Executive Edition, Atlanta, Georgia

Printed in the U.S.A.

Acknowledgments

Our sincere thanks to the Arthur and Elizabeth Schlesinger Library

on the History of Women in America at Radcliffe College, which

served as the inspiration for this series. We are grateful for the

unlimited access to its unique archives, as well as for the

assistance of its staff of curators and historians,

without whom this project would not have been possible.

Contents

Preface

It all started ten years ago with a phone call from the Director of the Schlesinger Library on the History of Women in America, requesting the video tapes of a television series I had produced and hosted called WOMAN TO WOMAN.

"Imagine these tapes as video diaries," Pat King responded to my surprised inquiry as to the purpose of her request. "Future generations will see and hear women talking about their lives, their work, their children and communities, and as modern women are regrettably keeping fewer diaries, writing fewer letters, there will be fewer written words and more need for other kinds of documentation."

To think of television in the same thought as books, libraries, and archives—and with a future beyond ratings cycles—was a new and wonderful concept to me. All it took was one visit to the Schlesinger, one amazing journey through its treasures of women's stories, to transform me into a woman with a mission: I wanted to find a way to use television, the modern archive, to further the mission of the Schlesinger, which had been established fifty years ago for the purpose of documenting and celebrating American women's lives and accomplishments. A fortunate few would come to the Schlesinger, as I had, and discover for themselves the often untold truth of how "women held up half the sky." A television series could share the good news with millions more.

Good idea. Tough sell. It took a decade of doubters before a young development executive at Turner Broadcasting, Vivian Schiller, got it. So did her boss. Thank you, Vivian—and your daughter, conceived during production, will thank you, too—for giving A CENTURY OF WOMEN its first, all-important *yes!*, and for the careful, caring supervision of the television series and this book.

Many more yeses followed from Terry Segal, Executive Vice President/General Manager of TBS Superstation, who never wavered in his total support for this project. Thanks, Terry, for your complete understanding of the project's significance, and, especially, for sharing my conviction that a CENTURY OF WOMEN book was important, too. It completes the dream, and you—more than most—believe in dreams.

Ted Turner believes in taking risks...and in doing the right thing. He did both in saying "yes" to funding and broadcasting A CENTURY OF WOMEN. Ted's a history buff and he was committed to telling an untold part of ours. Thanks, Ted, for this gift of history.

And to Jane Fonda—truly one of the great women of the twentieth century, in whose life and work are mirrored so many of our collective dreams and values—a great big personal thanks for so much more than the voice of A CENTURY OF WOMEN. You are also its soul and, for me as well as for many, many other women, a personal hero.

To Jacoba Atlas, whose words and creative vision brought the stories to life; to Diana, Lynne, Heidi, Kyra, Susan, Carol, Barbara, Chris, Sylvia, and Judy, plus a hundred or so other talented television professionals, my greatest admiration and appreciation. For the celebrated women from every walk of life who shared their memories, their personal stories, their insights, and their reflections, we are grateful and proud to be associated with you.

To Eva, Barbara, Diane, Sylvia, Ruth, the indominable Joan Challinor, and all the members of the Schlesinger's Advisory Board, many thanks for believing, too, and for the unabashed enthusiasm along the way.

Sadly, Pat King, who walked every step of the journey quietly and consistently encouraging, did not live to share in the joys of our mission accomplished. But each time this book is read or the video tapes are watched, Pat King will be honored. Thank you, Pat, for the gift of history you inspired with that first "imagine."

—Pat Mitchell

Once upon a time there was a visionary who had a modern dream. In the dream were many, many women heroes of every race and generation in a hundred years' time; the heroes overcame the ogres who hoarded the national treasure of freedom and they defeated dragons of ignorance, apathy, and hate. But no one knew who they were.

The visionary was a documentary filmmaker named Pat Mitchell and her modern dream was a book and a six-hour television series on TBS telling the stories of these heroes. Then she became an executive at TBS and she was encouraged by Jane Fonda, whose support was essential. And the dream was made visible.

VU Productions created a six-hour documentary. Women historians nourished it, women writers and researchers and filmmakers gave it substance. (Like the Marines, it also had a few good men: Ted Turner, Gary Goldberg, Scott Sassa.)

Women's history, Gloria Steinem reminds us, is lost and rediscovered, and lost and rediscovered, over and over again. The loss is ours, for these are tales of passions and tempers and plots and adventures of our country and our families—all of us, men and women. And women's history is part of the legacy that our daughters and sons must receive if they are to achieve their own dreams of behaving boldly and honorably in this world.

—Diana Meehan

MAY 1994

*I*ntroduction

⋆⋅⋅⫘⋅⋅⋆

During this century, women in America have pried open the closed door of the Democracy, squeezed inside, and established a space of their own. Many of us today are unaware of what it took to get there: the seemingly overwhelming obstacles and powerful resistance that were overcome, and the humor and inventiveness that often gave our foremothers a winning edge, like Margaret Sanger floating boxes full of diaphragms in empty brandy bottles into New York harbor.

It is because of the heroic acts of a multitude of women that today we have more life choices than ever before. If we choose to work, we can work under better conditions and receive better pay because of Pauline Newman, Jo Carol LaFleur, and Ida May Phillips. If we choose to stay at home and raise a family, we can do that more efficiently and with a greater sense of the value of our work because of Charlotte Perkins Gilman, Christine Frederick, and Alice McClellan Birney. If we want to break out and be different, Amelia Earhart, Dr. Mary Walker, and Edna St. Vincent Millay have made it okay. If we question whether women really do have a unique voice to cast out to the world, Judy Chicago, Georgia O'Keeffe, Willa Cather, Zora Neale Hurston, and Maya Angelou show us that, yes, we do see and hear things differently, and there's value in our expressions. If we don't like what our government is doing, we can run for office, as fifty-four of us did for the House and Senate in 1992, and we can win. Women like suffragist Alice Paul and Civil Rights Activist Fannie Lou Hamer made this possible.

The fact that the names of most of these women are unfamiliar should give us pause. We can learn so many important lessons from their stories: that one brave, committed woman can change history, that change doesn't happen overnight, that we should never give up. When we need strength and insight we have incredible role models to draw from, and in the years ahead we're going to need all the strength and insight we can muster.

Despite all the progress of the past one hundred years, there's still a lot left to be done. Debates about the rights and capabilities of women continue. Salaries and equal rights in the workplace are still, in many environments, things of the future. Questions of how to balance work and family and what a real partnership in the home should look like are still a source of anguish and confusion for many. But the more we understand about where we come from and why, the better we'll be able to understand where we are going and how we are going to get there.

So let's treat ourselves to our own history, the bedtime stories we were never told.

—Jane Fonda

A Century of Women

PART ONE

Work & Family

T*he conflict between work and family has affected all women, in the way they have been perceived, and the way they have perceived themselves. As labor reformers and feminists throughout the century applied pressure for equality both in the workplace and at home, many women found that the ebb and flow of job opportunities gradually led toward a wider range of career possibilities. Yet women workers were accused of taking jobs away from men, or of being deficient wives and mothers. While many women needed to work to support their families, their husbands offered them little relief from the toils of housework and parenting. Women sought to streamline home labors while trying to achieve recognition and status for their dual careers outside and inside the home.*

"Work & Family" analyzes the central and enduring conflict of women's lives, narrated through the voices of historical participants and contemporary witnesses such as Susan Ware, Charlotte Perkins Gilman, Betty Friedan, Elaine Jones, and Hillary Rodham Clinton.

CHAPTER ONE

The Great Uprising

"One of the constants of the twentieth century in women's lives has been the struggle between work and family—the roles that women want to play in their families and the role that they often need to play as paid workers.

"The ironic thing is that most of the women who were working at this time were not working because they wanted to or for personal fulfillment. They were working because they had to."

—Susan Ware,
historian

auline Newman was one of nearly five hundred girls who worked at the Triangle Shirtwaist Factory, a New York City dress manufacturer known for its miserable working conditions. Families needed their children's wages to make ends meet.

At the beginning of the twentieth century, newly arrived immigrants and other working class families could not afford the luxury of only one breadwinner. It wasn't a matter of choice, women had to work. Some labored at home with their children at their sides doing piecework. Others went into the factories.

"All the shops were as bad as the Triangle Waist Company. When you were told Saturday afternoons through a sign on the elevator, IF YOU DON'T COME IN ON SUNDAY, YOU NEEDN'T COME IN ON MONDAY! what choice did you have? You had no choice."

—Pauline Newman,
labor activist

"From where I sat I could see the children play and hear them singing. It was summer and the air in the shop was stuffy and hot. Often I longed to join the youngsters in the park and to breathe the cool fresh air....

"After all, I was not much older than they were!

"At the end of my first day's work, I was handed a slip of paper showing that I had earned thirty-five cents....

"I lived in a two-room tenement with my mother and two sisters, and the bedroom had no windows.... The facilities were down in the yard. In the summer, the sidewalk, fire escapes, and the roof of the tenements became bedrooms just to get a breath of fresh air. We wore cheap clothes, lived in cheap tenements, and ate cheap food. There was nothing to look forward to except the next day being better."

—Pauline Newman

Top: *At the turn of the century, children worked as adults inside mills.* **Overleaf:** *Professional women march down Fifth Avenue with banners declaring their occupations, 1913.* **Opposite page, top:** *Immigrants arrive at Ellis Island, New York, 1902.*

"At the turn of the century the trade unions consisted of relatively skilled men, whose hope was that women, all women, would be able to stay at home. And given how hard the lives were of women who both worked and had families, that was not an unreasonable expectation or hope."

—Alice Kessler Harris
historian

By the end of the century's first decade, conditions inside garment factories were intolerable. Workers saw their salaries cut and their hours increased. Women and children worked from morning until night, repeating the same menial tasks over and over again each day. When men worked in the factories, their positions were usually higher and their wages better.

In response, women tried to form a union.

The owners fought back.

"The tactics that were used by the employers in those days were not genteel, and there were no laws or rules that prevented them from physically attacking women. The woman who actually energized the strike vote and got the strike vote passed, Clara Lemlich, had herself been beaten up and assaulted and jailed for walking on a picket line."

—Alice Kessler Harris

In 1900, the average life expectancy for women was forty-three. Raising children was a life-long occupation. Only economic necessity forced wives and mothers from their homes.

On November 22, 1909, garment workers gathered at Cooper Union Hall. As labor leader Samuel Gompers addressed the crowd, Clara Lemlich rose and spoke out:

"Mr. Chairman, I am a working girl, one of those who is on strike against intolerable conditions. I am tired of listening to speakers who talk in general terms. What we are here for is to decide whether we shall or shall not strike. I offer a resolution that a general strike be declared now. We are starving while we work; we may as well starve while we strike!"

The strike, called "The Great Uprising," paralyzed New York City. The strikers were mostly young, unmarried women, still in their teens. Pauline Newman joined the picket line.

"During the weeks and months of the strike, most of them would go hungry. Many of them would find themselves without a roof over their heads. All of them would be cold and lonely. But all of them also knew and understood that their own courage would warm them, that hope for a better life would feed them, that fortitude would shelter them, that their fight for a better life would lift their spirits."

—Pauline Newman

This fight united women from all walks of life. A few society women crossed class lines and put up their mansions as bail for the hundreds who were arrested during the strike.

Mrs. Alva Belmont, known in the papers as Mrs. O. H. P. Belmont, was one of the society matrons actively supporting the strikers. She had been married to one America's most famous millionaires, William K. Vanderbilt, whom she divorced after she learned of his affair with a younger woman. When asked why she supported working class women, Mrs. Belmont said, flippantly,

"I do it to annoy my former husband, Mr. Vanderbilt."

The strike lasted months, cutting heavily into garment industry profits. Finally, many factory owners were willing to compromise, and wages were increased at some shops. But at the Triangle Shirtwaist Factory, there was no reason to celebrate. When workers at Triangle returned to their machines, they learned their wages were reduced, and their hours cut. Girls were also fined for talking or using the toilet. Doors were locked to keep the workers inside and union organizers out. It was a blueprint for disaster.

Top: *Thousands of women join the Triangle Shirtwaist strikers, New York, 1909.*
Opposite page, bottom left: *Labor leader Samuel Gompers addresses garment workers at Cooper Union Hall, 1909.* **Opposite page, inset:** *Clara Lemlich*

THE NEW [Y...]

NEW YORK, SUNDAY, MARCH 26, 1911.—112 PAGES

[O]NE HUNDRED AND FIFTY PERISH I[N]
WOMEN AND GIRLS, TRAPPED IN
LOST IN FLAMES OR HUR[...]

Fire broke out at the Triangle Shirtwaist Factory on Saturday, March 25, 1911. Within minutes, the deadly blaze was completely out of control. Nearly five hundred women and girls were trapped behind locked doors on the seventh, eighth, and ninth floors. Firemen arrived quickly, but rescue attempts failed—their ladders reached only as high as the sixth floor.

FACTORY FIRE;
EN STORY BUILDING,
THEMSELVES TO DE.

OFFICES
SHOW ROOMS
AND
SHIPPING
DEPARTMENTS

BUILDING AT NORTH-WEST CORNER OF
WASHINGTON PLACE AND GREENE ST
THREE TOP FLOORS IN WHICH LOSS

James Cooper, a reporter for the New York *World-Telegram*, witnessed the tragedy:

"A young man helped a girl to the window on the ninth floor. Then he held her out deliberately away from the building and let her drop. He held out a second girl the same way and let her drop. He held out a third girl who did not resist. There were as unresisting as if he were helping them into a streetcar instead of eternity...."

One hundred and forty-six young women and three men died—burned to death or killed when they jumped from windows in a desperate attempt to cheat the flames. Their average age—nineteen.

Above: Relatives identify victims of the Triangle Shirtwaist fire, 1911.

Pauline Newman escaped the inferno. Shortly before the fire, she had left her job at the Triangle Shirtwaist Factory to work full-time as a labor organizer. She was one of thousands of mourners who marched down Fifth Avenue remembering their fallen sisters.

"Everybody was marching. It seemed the entire city was on the march.

"It was raining, but no one cared. It was something I'll never forget. Thousands of people stood in the rain.

"It looked like the entire city of New York was at the parade, if you could call it a parade. And it was pouring. It was as if nature were weeping."
—Pauline Newman

Rose Schneiderman, a union activist and close friend of Pauline Newman's, spoke for many women:

"This is not the first time girls have been burned alive in the city. Every week I must learn of the untimely death of one of my sister workers. The life of men and women is so cheap and property is sacred. Too much blood has been shed.

"I know from experience it is up to the working people to save themselves. The only way they can save themselves is by a strong working-class movement."

Right: Rose Schneiderman, Clara Lemlich, and Pauline Newman would remain lifelong friends and would work together to improve the conditions of working women throughout America. Opposite page, middle: Suffrage lobbyists in Washington, D.C.

Women had another dynamic heroine in Elizabeth Gurley Flynn. She was called the Joan of Arc of labor in tribute to her remarkable courage.

Flynn traveled the country organizing workers, often with her baby son in her arms. She was a fiery speaker and a tireless advocate for decent working conditions. Her daring was celebrated in song.

In 1912, Flynn arrived in Lawrence, Massachusetts. There, workers from the textile mills had begun to strike. The Lawrence strike would prove to be one of the most important for American labor, with profound repercussions for working women. In this crucible, wives and mothers would demand and receive recognition as union leaders and would take their grievances all the way to Capitol Hill.

"The women worked in the mills for lower pay and in addition had all the housework and the care of the children. The old-world attitude of man as lord and master was strong. At the end of a day's work—now of strike duty—the man went home and sat at ease while his wife did all the work preparing the meal, cleaning the house."
—Elizabeth Gurley Flynn,
labor activist

Elizabeth Gurley Flynn, herself a mother, understood women's unique predicament:

"Pregnant women worked at the machines until a few hours before their babies were born. Sometimes a baby came right there in the mill, between the looms."

Women wanted respect, not only as workers, but for the double duty they put in—first working in the mills all day, then going home to what would be called, in future generations, "The Second Shift."

There was considerable male opposition in Lawrence to women going to meetings and marching on the picket lines.

"We set out to combat these notions. The women wanted to picket. They were strikers as well as wives and were valiant fighters."
—Elizabeth Gurley Flynn

"The men went around saying, you know, 'These are just poor, weak women and how could weak women stay out on strike? It takes a tough man to do that.' And, after all, other women were getting beaten up on the picket lines."
—Alice Kessler Harris

On February 19, 1912, two hundred police drew their clubs and went after one hundred women, knocking them to the ground and beating them. The violence was so intense, strike leaders urged the women to stay home and off the picket line. They refused.

As the strike wore on, there was even less food than usual for the children. Mill women appealed to mothers across America to help and many families volunteered to take in the hungry children of the Lawrence strikers.

Strikers reluctantly sent their children away on trains to the food and safety of these surrogate families. But one group of children did not escape Lawrence unharmed.

*Bottom: Strikers and Massachusetts militia face off, Lawrence, 1912. **Opposite page, top:** Lawrence children wait to be railed to safety. **Opposite page, bottom:** Militia soldier with billy club, 1912.*

"Just as they were ready to board the train, they were surrounded by the police. Children were clubbed and torn away from their mothers, and a wild scene of brutal disorder took place.

"Thirty-five women and children were arrested. They were beaten into submission and taken to the patrol station.

"They tore down that railroad station later. And I'm sure one reason is that they didn't want people to be pointing it out as the place where the police and soldiers had beaten the women and children.

"The result was a Congressional investigation....

"There were sixteen witnesses down there before that committee—children. And every one of those children was actually a worker in the mills."

—Elizabeth Gurley Flynn

William M. Wood

The conditions exposed in Lawrence so shocked the nation that William M. Wood, owner of the American Woolen Company, was forced to settle the strike.

Contributions women made to the victory at Lawrence earned them the respect of union leaders as well as the appreciation of their husbands.

Elizabeth Gurley Flynn would go on to other strikes, and she continued to speak out for workers' rights until her death in 1963.

Rose Schneiderman

"What the woman who labors wants is the right to live, not simply to exist, the right to life as the rich woman has it, the right to life, and the sun and music and art.

"You have nothing that the humblest worker has not a right to have also. The worker must have bread, but she must have roses too."

—Rose Schneiderman,
labor activist

CHAPTER TWO

Children or Careers?

"The great trouble is that most people confuse motherhood with housework. The least efficient, most wasteful labor is that of every man for himself. The next lowest is every woman for her man.

"If they were not women, these innumerable cooks, this fifty percent of the human race deliberately set aside to cook for the other fifty, no sane economist could bear the thought of such a colossal waste of labor."

— Charlotte Perkins Gilman, author

Above: Radcliffe students, 1916. **Opposite page:** Alice McClellan Birney and her children.

J ust before the turn of the century, while working-class women were struggling for higher wages and better working conditions, another class of people were involved in a very different experience. Alice Birney, a businesswoman and mother, was cheered by the progress women were making outside the home, but she still believed a woman's most important work was motherhood.

Birney had been widowed while expecting her first child. She struggled to educate herself, but questioned whether the college education that more and more women were getting truly contributed to a woman's ability to raise children.

"To the average woman, no field affords such opportunities for royal and lasting services to humanity and to our present and future civilization, as that which lies within the four walls of the home.

"This is a time known pre-eminently in the history of the world as the woman's era. So much has been said and written in these latter days about the higher education, the extended opportunities for women, that we have failed to hear the still, small voice of childhood. And yet, how, I ask, can we divorce the woman question from the child question? Is not the one the natural, logical corollary of the other?"

—Alice McClellan Birney

Phoebe Hearst

"The higher branches of book learning are well enough for the girl or woman who has the inclination or time for them, but they should be secondary in her education to the knowledge which shall fit her for motherhood."

—Alice McClellan Birney

Birney, who would remarry and have two more children, devoted her life to making the world a better place for children. She organized the first Mothers Congress in Washington, D.C. The agenda: improved schools, healthier children, and stronger families.

Birney offered the vision, and the matriarch of the Hearst publishing family, Mrs. Phoebe Hearst, provided the money. Together they gathered research on child-rearing and created clubs where mothers could share their experiences and work together with educators for the betterment of their children. Eventually this would turn into the Parent-Teacher Association, or PTA.

Children or careers, women could not have both.

At least, that's what many people thought.

This choice to limit families troubled many women, including writer and reformer Charlotte Perkins Gilman.

When Gilman said, "Motherhood is a woman's first duty," there was irony in her words, because as a young woman she had struggled with conventional expectations.

Gilman was raised in poverty by her mother; her father had abandoned the family. In her early twenties, she was courted by a painter named Charles Walter Stetson. She agonized over whether she should marry him, knowing that she had work to do in the world, and that marriage and motherhood could be confining.

Despite her qualms, she and Stetson married, but their union was troubled from the beginning. When they divorced, Gilman gave up custody of her daughter. For that decision, she would be publicly criticized throughout the rest of her life.

Eventually, Gilman remarried—to her first cousin and childhood friend, Houghton Gilman.

"These nervous troubles are dreadfully depressing. John does not know how much I really suffer. He knows there is no reason to suffer and that satisfies him....

"Of course it is fortunate Mary is so good with the baby. Such a dear baby! And yet I cannot be with him, it makes me so nervous...."

—Charlotte Perkins Gilman,
"The Yellow Wallpaper"

Analytical and witty, Charlotte Perkins Gilman was one of the first to cast a sharp eye on the relationship between men and women. She then devised a blueprint for a more equitable way of cohabitating.

"Every man, to the poorest, thinks he must have one whole woman to cook for him, and they both think it is economical.

"If each man did for himself the work he expects of his woman, there would be no wealth in the world, only millions and millions of poor, tired men.

"As things are now, a man marries a woman loving and revering her, but on account of woman's dependence on man, she has to do the housework and becomes merely his domestic, his cook.

"What man can revere his cook? But, you may say, the man works for her: why should she not work for him?

"It is not true. The man works for the world and the world pays him for his work, which the man uses to support the woman who works for him.

"The whole thing boils itself down to the fact that if the man dies, the woman loses her job. The element of waste has not been considered because we are not accustomed to women's work as having any cash value."

—*Charlotte Perkins Gilman*

① ①

Sept. 19th 1891.
about 27 items.
1800 word.

The Question of Life for the Married Woman.

Unless the question of life can be answered for the married woman it is not answered at all. For the adult woman is the type of race, and marriage, of some sort, is an essential condition of existence.

What the girl does is temporarily useful, and has some lasting effects, what the unmarried woman does is widely useful but not transmitted to descendants, what the married woman does — what Woman does — as a whole.

Here is where we meet the whole woman question. The Home — The Family — The Sacred ties of Wifehood and Motherhood — the claims that are held to interfere with her development.

Mrs. C. P. Stetson
1673 Grove St. Oakland
Cal.

Economic Side of Marriage

[We are] probably all more or less familiar [with the] history of that human institution [of] marriage. It is human purely, [we are] distinctly told that in heaven [is] neither marrying nor given in marriage.

[Whi]le admitting our vague general [ideas] on the subject, I would like to [make] a definition before we enter on it[s discussion].

[What] is marriage? [In wha]t does it essentially consist? [Turni]ng to the dictionary I find [I] use the word wedlock or mat[rimony], [you] marriage referring more to [the fact] that than to the state, though [u]sed for the latter.

The state of which I am speaking [marri]age is a civil contract, matrimony

"Housewives' Lament"

It's sweeping at six,

and it's dusting at seven.

It's victuals at eight,

and the dishes at nine.

It's potting and panning

from ten to eleven.

We scarce break our fast

till we plan how to dine.

Children or Careers?   ———   25

Most middle-class women received a housekeeping allowance from their husbands. Economic dependence meant social and political dependence as well.

Suffragist and journalist Rebecca Hourwich was reminded of just what that meant when she and a Mrs. Havermeyer tried to raise money to gain women the vote.

> MRS. HAVERMEYER: *"Will you give us a hundred?"*
> HOSTESS: *"No, I'm afraid I couldn't afford that."*
> MRS. HAVERMEYER: *"But perhaps you could give us ten dollars a month."*
> HOSTESS (ALMOST IN TEARS): *"Well, I'm afraid I can't do that either."*
> MRS. HAVERMEYER: *"Well, couldn't you do it out of your vegetable money?"*
> HOSTESS (APOLOGETICALLY): *"I don't think you understand, Mrs. Havermeyer. I write the checks; my husband signs them. I don't see five dollars in cash from one month to another, and if my husband doesn't approve of what I write in my checkbook, he either won't pay it, or I don't do it again. I could never give you a monthly pledge because he doesn't approve of what you are doing."*

Christine Frederick, on the other hand, didn't want to *escape* homemaking, she wanted to *dignify* it.

Frederick said that homemaking was a "fine antidote to the unnatural cravings for a career," without ever acknowledging, of course, that a career was precisely what she had.

Frederick had four children and a good education. She would put both to use. She moved to Long Island in 1910 and converted several rooms of her house into a model of the future home, showcasing what modern appliances could do. She called her project "The Applecroft Home Experiment Station."

Below: Christine Frederick with three of her children, 1927. **Opposite page:** *Time-motion studies at the Applecroft Home Experiment Station.*

"Women should dissolve the bonds that have shackled them to drudgery and declare homemaking a recognized profession."
—Christine Frederick

"Women have not let machinery serve them. If women can operate machinery so successfully in the factory, why are they not willing to try it in the household, where it will save them untold effort, labor, and time?

—Christine Frederick

Frederick's idea was to apply the principals of scientific management to basic housework: "If only she buys the right labor savers and learns to use them properly..."

...labor savers like mechanical dishwashers and washing machines. Frederick studied household tools and methods meticulously to see where improvements could be made, and tasks simplified.

"...The most precious possession of the housewife in these days is time. It is not necessary for the care of the household to take the full time of any woman.

"The reason housework is generally an all-day, ten- or twelve-hour job is because THE WOMAN HERSELF DOESN'T PLAN."

—Christine Frederick

"Where's the drainer? How high is the sink? How tall is the worker? Does she stand or sit? Where's the pantry? One rinse or two? How long did it take?"

—Christine Frederick

Until her death in 1970, Frederick wrote advice columns and books that were directed exclusively at the growing middle class. She was the first in a long line of experts to instruct women on the "feminine arts." It was the beginning of the home economics movement.

"No need for the bride to feel tragic,
The rest is push-button magic.
So whether you bake or broil or stew,
The Frigidaire kitchen does it all for you!
Don't have to be chained to the stove all day.
Just set the timer and you're on your way."

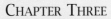

CHAPTER THREE

The Domestic Revolution

"Above all, I ask you in the name of humanity that we be helped to help ourselves before we are absolutely destitute. Could you instruct us where to apply and secure work—any kind, any wage, anywhere?"

—letter to Franklin Delano Roosevelt
from a woman named
Daisy Hitch Davies
during the Depression

The Great Depression put millions out of work. Any progress women had made in the first thirty years of the century was cut short by the crushing reality of hard times.

The public perception of those out of work during the Depression was that they were all men. Women were assumed to have a husband, father, or brother to take care of them, but, in reality, many women were heads of households with no means of support.

Women were looking for work, and relying on handouts. The government dole helped many survive, but it was not enough.

"It is one of the great mysteries of the city where women go when they're out of work and hungry. There are not many women in the bread line. There are no flop houses for women as there are for men, where a bed can be had for a quarter or less. They obviously don't sleep in the jungle or under the newspapers in the park. There is no law, I suppose, against them being in those places, but the fact is, they rarely are."

—Meridel LeSueur,
journalist

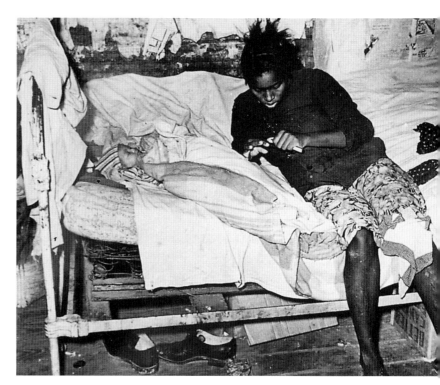

Government programs were put in place to give people jobs. But there was a catch. As the Depression ate away at people's purses and pride, women were accused of robbing men of the jobs they needed.

Women who had jobs were fired, and many states refused to hire married women. To make matters worse, in 1932, the government said there could be only one government job per family. Women whose husbands worked for the government also were fired.

Frances Perkins, FDR's Secretary of Labor, was the first woman to hold a position in a president's cabinet. As a young woman she had campaigned for suffrage and supported union efforts to better conditions for workers. Of course she supported working women, but when it came to public policy, her hands were tied:

"It is a well-known secret that married women just took off their wedding rings and pretended to be single. How else can you account for the actual increase in the number of married women working during the Depression?

"But we had no choice in the Federal government but to limit one job per family. It was meant to discourage nepotism, but it discriminated against women."

Frances Perkins went to court to keep her own name after she married and had a daughter:

"I suppose I had been somewhat touched by feminist ideas and that was the reason I kept my maiden name. My whole generation was, I suppose, the first generation that openly and actively asserted—at least some did—the separateness of women and their personal independence in family relationships."

Top: *Secretary of Labor Frances Perkins was the first woman to serve in a president's cabinet.* **Right:** *Perkins with her daughter Suzanne.*

Women took any job they could, but options were limited, especially for black women. The leading occupation for them was domestic worker. And by the 1930s, as hard times paralyzed America, most domestic workers in the country were black.

"During the Depression period, there was something in the Bronx, New York, called the slave market. When people were very desperate and out of work, they would go to empty lots in the Bronx, where white women would come and make the black women underbid each other for services for a days work."

—Paula Giddings,
historian

"I wonder why it is that the same God who made us, made the rest of mankind, and yet, when it comes to hours and wages, there is such a difference."

—Serena Ashford,
cook

The New Deal social programs, like minimum wage laws, excluded domestic workers. This exclusion angered many women.

On the West Coast, canneries offered low-paying, mind-numbing work that often went to Mexican Americans. Despite a culture that revered the sanctity of the home, wives, mothers, and grandmothers toiled in canneries to help their families survive.

> "When you're talking about family life among Mexican cannery workers in California during the 1930s, you're looking particularly at women's experience.
> "It was necessary for families to pool their income. It's what historians called 'the family wage economy.'"
>
> —Vicki Ruiz,
> historian

As the Depression deepened, workers across America struck for better pay. Auto workers, steel workers, and meat packers all walked picket lines. Women working in the successful cannery plants in California went on strike.

In Los Angeles, children carried signs which read "I'm under-fed because my Mama is underpaid."

Within twenty-four hours, the strike at the Shapiro Cannery was settled. Latina women had earned a major economic victory for themselves and their families.

"Cannery,"
by Carmen Tafolla

The whistle of the cannery breaks the night,

stealing sleep and breath and dreams

from half-grown children Mama needs to

rouse to dress and run down to the

cannery to meet the boatload of sardines.

Gramma's joints are stiff, I can tell,

her knees tired of the weight

and aching with the blackness of the

> *morning,*

as Papa's back bends further over, to

> *work faster,*

Lupe's fresh red cut from yesterday's

> *slash-to-the-bone*

shies away from the slap of sardines,

but she forces it back.

Juana's wishing we had higher pay

and Anita's just wishing she could play.

Do the job HE left behind

APPLY U.S. EMPLOYMENT SE

On December 7, 1941, the bombing of Pearl Harbor forced the United States into war with Japan. America's entrance into World War II effectively ended the Depression. Men went off to fight and, for the first time in more than a decade, there were more jobs than workers.

Enter: the women.

"More and more men are being called into the armed forces. Their jobs must be filled and filled now. And who can fill them? You! You women, you're the ones who must fill them, who can give our boys what they need. A thousand more planes, and more and more tanks. More and more guns and more ships."

—*from the film* Wanted: Women War Workers
from the office of war information

After decades of telling women their duty was to stay home and take care of their children, there was a new message:
GET A JOB!

Right: *Women sealers work on the U.S.S. George Washington Carver, World War II.*

Tina Hill had been a maid in Tyler, Texas, before moving west, aiming for a better life. When she was hired for war work at North American Aircraft in Los Angeles, it was the start of a thirty-five-year career.

"The war opened up jobs for women; it gave them a chance to work and earn a decent living. The black woman has always had to go out and work, but the war really made it more acceptable.

"The pay was good, that was the main thing. The pay was good."

—Tina Hill

"World War II was a very important era for black women workers—for all women workers in fact—because of course they had the opportunity for the first time really in large numbers, white women particularly, to move into the labor force.

"There were more and more opportunities for black and white women to work side by side as well, even though there was a great deal of racism that remained."

—Paula Giddings

"I've always said that it's the mighty ill wind that don't blow someone some good. So by Hitler starting the war, that helped the black woman out of the white woman's kitchen."

—Tina Hill

Three million women—black, white, Asian American, Latina—went to work in defense plants throughout the country. Another 350,000 women joined the military. In 1942, the Women's Auxiliary Army Corps, the WAACs, sent women to the front lines.

Mothers working in defense plants had to figure out what to do with their children. Most formed babysitting collectives because the government-promised daycare rarely materialized.

Women discovered that working outside the home could be fun and rewarding. Their image was both patriotic and glamorous. It was the makings of a revolution on the homefront.

Not everything was rosey for women at home during the war. For many, a very different story was unfolding.

"For Japanese American women and men alike, World War II was a disillusioning and difficult time. They lost their freedom, their civil liberties, their homes, businesses, and neighborhoods.
"More than a hundred and ten thousand men, women, and children were uprooted from communities throughout the West and incarcerated in internment camps in very desolate regions of the interior."
—Valerie Matsumoto,
historian

"I was very disillusioned at the time and I think even more so when I saw what Manzanar was like. It was kind of a shock to be moved so far away, and then to find that we were going to have barbed wire around us and a guard tower and a sentry and a machine gun and a search light.
"And I think that all of us really were devastated by that.... American citizenship didn't mean anything at that point."
—Sue Embrey,
former internment camp inmate

"People often ask, 'What was it like?' Physically, it was tolerable, but psychologically I think we were all traumatized to the point where you knew you were there for a reason that seemed unfathomable to us at that time."
—Mitsuye Yamada,
former internment camp inmate

Internment camps like Manzanar in California prompted the breakdown of the traditional patriarchal Japanese family. Many *Nisei*—second generation Americans—were allowed to leave the internment camps to attend college in the midwest and east.

Ironically the suspension of parents' civil rights resulted in unprecedented opportunities for their daughters.

"My mother was quite strict in maintaining a certain decorum in the community, so I doubt very much if she would have permitted me to leave and run off to college. But the circumstances in camp, I think, allowed me to do that."

—Mitsuye Yamada

Even here, in such unfair and unhappy circumstances, the wives and mothers who stayed behind tried to make camp life bearable.

"As the months went by, you found more and more people planting things and forming groups so that people could get together forming baseball teams and whatever. So that Manzanar really became a very beautiful place after a year of building and, in the end, it was a small American community. But that was all we knew, was to live like Americans."

—Sue Embrey

Top: *A Japanese American family inside a tent home, Nyssa, Oregon, 1942.* **Opposite page, bottom:** *Manzanar internment camp, California, during World War II.*

After the war, as the victory champagne was uncorked and there was dancing in the streets, the Labor Department's Women's Bureau surveyed the new women working in industry.

Seventy-five percent of all of them, and ninety percent of black women, planned to work *after* the war. They said they liked the work…and liked the money.

"When my husband came home from the war, he couldn't tell me to stay home because I had gotten accustomed to working and making money, and making my own decisions. So I couldn't go backwards; I had to go forwards."

—*Tina Hill*

America had a problem....

CHAPTER FOUR

The Problem That Had No Name

"By putting a name to the problem, by making it public, I realized that each woman alone who wasn't having an orgasm waxing the kitchen floor was not isolated, not suffering from some grievous sin, but suffering some shared, common socio-economic-psychological problem with other women.

"I then had to look into the history of the vote, which had been blotted out of history, and I discovered that these women were not neurotic, man-eating, penis-envy monsters, but the passionate women that they were."

—Betty Friedan

W omen who had bucked the rivets in the bombers and worked the assembly lines woke up the morning after the war ended... and were handed pink slips.

"When the war ends, once again you have another reversal and women are told that juvenile delinquency is a consequence of their going out to work. And now they better stay home and have babies and take care of their families, because their families have been neglected during the war."

—Alice Kessler Harris,
historian

Some women, out of necessity or choice, continued to work. The jobs open to them were mostly on the lower end of the payscale as secretaries, bookkeepers, sales clerks, teachers, or nurses. Without any public support and facing a good deal of criticism, women struggled to combine work and family life. Anthropologist Margaret Mead was one of those surveying the potential damage:

"Women and men in large numbers are confused, uncertain, and discontented with the present definition of women's place in America. If you are a man, your way of making a living is still a matter of choice; if you are a girl, it ultimately isn't.

"All are expected—because they fall in love and want to get married—to want also to be homemakers and to enjoy the routine of bringing up children."

If having their men back home wasn't as blissful as they'd daydreamed, women were advised by the *Ladies Home Journal* to seek marriage counseling so they could get their priorities straight:

> *"Sometimes it's as simple as showing a wife her ex-GI's accusation that she's a sloppy housekeeper is quite just, thereby sending her posthaste to one of the 13,156 centers for adult education in homemaking now available in the United States."*

It was the 1950s. Marriage rates soared, and birthrates, too, as families settled into the comfort of the suburbs. It was the life that became, for many, the American Dream.

When *Life Magazine* celebrated the American woman in 1956, it chose the suburban wife and mother as its ideal.

"The fifties was the perfect time to live. And to be a homemaker was the ideal life and I loved it.

"There was no such thing in those days as a career, per se. There were women out there working, but I didn't know about them."

—Marjorie Sutton,
homemaker

Marjorie Sutton was born and raised in California. Right after World War II, she married her high school sweetheart, and together they settled just south of Los Angeles to raise a family.

"All the girls, we got married after school and we went right into homemaking, and we learned as we went. We had so many things to do, so much. Each child was involved in different things. And they had school activities, and I had to be a mother at PTA.

"We were in Campfire Girls, and the boys were Boy Scouts. And we did all these things with the children....

"One of the best things in the world—I loved to pack lunches. And they went off to school happy little kids. Happy little campers.

"We thought it was wonderful because we had all the money we needed. My husband was learning his business; he was going up, as you would say, the corporate ladder, and everything went well."

—Marjorie Sutton

But life in suburbia had its drawbacks. Washing clothes wasn't as fascinating as advertisers would have had women believe. And the isolation of women left home all day with small children could be frustrating.

"It would be a tremendous threat to me, I feel, if I had to stay home constantly with her because I feel that I would become as insular as those mothers in the park.

"I heard a fifteen-minute dialogue on detergents which absolutely astounded me one day; I mean, it sounded like something out of a TV commercial. I couldn't believe people actually talked that way. And it's either that, or they talk about their children."

—from An Uneasy Life,
a 1962 documentary

"Well, here it is, Monday morning, girls, and while you're happily starting the weekly wash, I know that each and every one of you is inspired with the knowledge that you're engaged in the fascinating business of making a home."

Betty Friedan, a mother of three who lived in suburban New York, called it "the problem that had no name."

It was the notion that a woman's *only* place was at home...or in a maternity dress...or on a pedestal.

"All the stuff that was being written about the 'woman problem,' or blaming women for their husbands' ulcers, or their children's bed-wetting, or their lack of orgasms, or their not getting the kitchen sink pure white.

"But there was no name *for this problem that the woman would express when she said, 'I'm Dan's wife. I'm Junior and Janie's mom. I'm a maker of meals and putter-on of diapers and, you know, a chauffeur...*

"'But who am I? Who am I?'"
—*Betty Friedan,*
author

Betty Friedan's question hit a nerve among American women. In 1963, Friedan gave the problem a name. Her book *The Feminine Mystique* sold more than three hundred thousand copies in less than six months.

"Women heard about the book and there were cartoons about this red book—it had a red cover—and women had this great relief, you know. And they stopped me and they said, 'Oh, it changed my life, it changed my whole life. I remember where I was...'"
—*Betty Friedan*

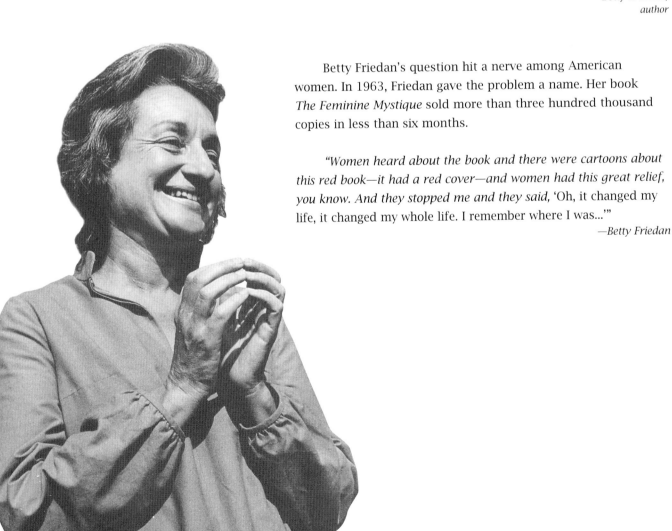

"By the time the 1950s and '60s hit, and Betty Friedan wrote The Feminine Mystique, *it was apparent that for much of a woman's married years, it was not at all necessary for her to stay in the home."*
—Alice Kessler Harris

In fact, the popular image of women as happy homemakers is misleading. By 1958, forty-three percent of all women were working outside the home. Most had jobs, not careers, and they worked to help make ends meet. Some were the sole support for their families.

"The juxtaposition of family and work is the constant theme in the twentieth century. Whether women neglect their families when they work, whether work inhibits women from being good mothers—those are the issues that have run the course of the twentieth century, and I think we haven't resolved them yet."

—Alice Kessler Harris

In post-World War II America, women turned their attention to other issues, issues that went far beyond their own family or community.

But their concerns were, in fact, rooted in both.

Below: "Women Strike for Peace" outside a Nevada Test Sight, 1962.

"When I left my teaching job to go start organizing farm workers, a lot of people thought I had just gone completely bananas."

—Dolores Huerta

In California, farm workers were also demanding justice. At the center of their struggle was Dolores Huerta, a teacher and mother of six.

Dolores Huerta was pregnant with her seventh child when Cesar Chavez called her to help him organize the United Farm Workers Union.

"When we had the first strike in 1965, I became a picket captain. I had a whole town that I was responsible for, and would go out at 3:00 in the morning and take everybody out to the picket line.

"But then the growers got injunctions on us, and then we all started getting arrested. And I was one of the first people to go to jail.

"When we saw that we couldn't win by striking any more, then we had to go out on a boycott.

"Having the women and the children on the picket line made it a lot easier to maintain the non-violent stance....

"The men always said, 'bring the women,' because the women would give them more, I don't know, encouragement. Because the picket line, if you're out there for eight or nine hours, can get very, very tiring. So having the women out there was a big boost, even for the men. And I think that's what made the Farm Workers Union very strong—because it's a family movement, you know, it includes everybody.

"The reason that I did all of this work—knowing that I had all of these children—was I knew that a lot of people were depending on me. And I always used to say in my prayers—if I'm not doing the right thing, I want a sign, you know, that I'm not doing the right thing, that I should stop what I'm doing and pay more attention to my children."

—Dolores Huerta

As first Vice President and principal negotiator, Huerta's leadership was crucial to the success of the United Farm Workers Union. Huerta's presence at the negotiating table forced men to confront the reality of what it meant to be a working mother.

"When I had my younger children and I was still negotiating, I would take nursing breaks. So I would take my baby into the negotiations and then I would take a nursing break, and everybody would have to wait while the baby ate. Then I would come back to the table to start negotiating again....

"I think it made employers sensitive to the fact that when we're talking about benefits and the terms of a contract, we're talking about families and we're talking about children."

—Dolores Huerta

Top: *Huerta protests working conditions at the Gallo Vineyards, 1973.* **Bottom:** *Dolores Huerta with Cesar Chavez, 1970.* **Opposite page:** *A triumphant Dolores Huerta at the United Farm Workers Union First Founding Convention, Fresno, California, 1962.*

Huerta's contribution helped better the lives of farm workers. Wages were increased, housing conditions improved, and fewer children worked in the fields.

Dolores Huerta had challenged many stereotypes with her important role and effective leadership. Latino women and men had a new kind of definition of wife and mother.

"As far as my children are concerned, they turned out well. They know how to fight for people, and how to fight for themselves. My oldest son's a doctor, but he works in a low-income area with farm workers; I have a son who's an attorney; several of my daughters are in the health field, and they work with low-income people. So my whole ideal has been for my children to be in a position where they can also serve others, and that is my reward."
—Dolores Huerta

Dolores Huerta's political work also helped give a voice to women; as they fought for equality for others, they began to question their own equality under the law. A legal revolution would be born.

CHAPTER FIVE

From Civil Rights to Equal Rights

"The law and public attitudes go together. Title VII says 'Thou shalt not discriminate on the basis of sex.' The year before, the Equal Pay Act said, 'Thou shalt not pay the women less than the men.' And people accept those norms as what's right and proper. So I think that the changing attitudes in society produce changes in the law. And the change in the law reinforces changing attitudes in society. I don't think there would have been a chance for the laws against sex discrimination if women had not begun to come alive and agitate for increased rights and opportunities. Then the law affirmed what the women were saying. And then people said, 'Well, that's the law.'"

—Ruth Bader Ginsburg,
Supreme Court Justice

*I*n 1961, the man in the White House knew that American women were at a crossroads:

"I see thousands of women getting out of colleges each year, and I wonder what happens to all these skills. What chance do they have to make full use of their powers?"

—*President John F. Kennedy*

President Kennedy appointed a Commission on the Status of Women. It was the first time in American history that the role of women became part of our national agenda.

In the late 1950s and early 1960s, more women than ever before were going to college, and most wanted more than just an MRS degree. But they were graduating into a world that had little use for their education, ambition, and commitment.

Equality on the work front was a long way off, even for a future Supreme Court Justice.

"I can best describe the way things were in my day as the closed door era. Women couldn't do this and women couldn't do that. In so many fields the door was just shut tight.

"I got out of law school in 1959. I began law school with a class of over four hundred. It included nine women. Employers were, to put it euphemistically, cool toward the idea of employing women. And I had three strikes against me. I was Jewish and the firms were just opening up to Jewish students. I was a woman. And I was a mother and that finished it. I had a four-year-old daughter and legal employers feared that I would be constantly running home to take care of my child and not be able to do the job.

"I didn't say anything. I accepted that that's the way it was, and I had to try harder and keep on until someone would employ me."

—*Ruth Bader Ginsburg*

Justice Ginsburg's experience was not unique. In the 1960s, job discrimination based solely on gender was widely accepted as appropriate.

At the same time, the issue of equality was galvanizing Americans. Women and men were taking to the streets demanding fair play. Ultimately the fight for Civil Rights would result in nothing less than a social revolution which would embrace women as well.

"You've got to remember that this is a nation of laws, and if something is not in the law, if it's not protected by the law, if it's not recognized by the law, then you don't have anything.

"That's why Title VII is so important. It's the first time in an employment law that women get access as a matter of law to full employment opportunities."

—*Elaine Jones,*
NAACP Legal Defense Fund

Top: Ruth Bader Ginsburg with her young daughter.
Bottom: Judge Ginsburg at her Senate Confirmation hearing for U.S. Supreme Court.

The first battlefield was Congress, where the Civil Rights Act was being debated, particularly Title VII of that Act, which would ban discrimination on the basis of "race, color, religion, or national origin."

An eighty-one-year-old Congressman from Virginia, Howard W. Smith, suggested that the word "sex" be added. He was certain that if he added "sex" to "race, color, and religion," Congress would view the whole proposition as ridiculous, and they would stop the Civil Rights Act cold.

"I have certainly tried to do everything that I could to hinder, delay, and dilapidate this bill."
—Howard W. Smith

Congresswoman Martha Griffith had another idea:
"When I got up to speak, the room was rocking with laughter and the first thing I said was, 'If there were any need to prove your disrespect, you've already proved it by your laughter.

"'We have sat here for four days discussing the rights of blacks and other minorities and there has been no laughter, not even a smile, but when you suggest that you shouldn't discriminate against your own wives, your own mothers, your own daughters, your own granddaughters, or your own sisters, then you laugh.'
"There was silence. Complete and absolute silence."

Congresswoman Griffith had, throughout her career, championed racial equality, but she was willing to play into the prejudices of the all-white House of Representatives so that women would have an equal chance as well.

"And then I said to them, 'You have succeeded in dividing American labor into three parts. First are American white men, who stand at the top and will get what they've always gotten. Then you are going to put in black men and women, and the third class will be your mothers, your wives, your widows, your daughters, and your sisters. They will be the last hired and the first fired. Why are you doing this? Add "sex." Why discriminate against white women?'
"Well, that did it."

In 1964, Congress passed, and President Johnson signed, the Civil Rights Act. Title VII included the word "sex." For the first time in American history, job discrimination against women was illegal.

"The Civil Rights Act of 1964 is one of the most effective legal weapons that women have had during this century. What that Act gave us was the right to work, and to be hired, and to be promoted, without regard to our gender. Women now had a tool. It's very important to have a tool with which to work, but then you need lawyers and you need people who are willing to complain. You need women who are willing to stand up and say 'I have been wronged, and I'm going to court to vindicate my rights.'"
—Elaine Jones

The first woman to stand up and fight was a single mother with seven children looking for a way to change her life. Ida May Phillips was a waitress in Florida, barely getting by, when she saw an ad for assembly trainees at the Martin-Marietta company.

"They would not accept her application, and the reason is she had preschool-age children. It was the corporation's view that she should be in the home, rather than in the workplace. Yet, men with preschool-age children, their applications were accepted and they were hired."

—Elaine Jones

Ida May Phillips

Ida May Phillips was outraged. She knew what many American women knew—that working was a necessity, not a choice. She sued, citing Title VII of the Civil Rights Act.

"If I win my case, it will mean that I would have a job, that I would have regular hours in order to plan things with my family. It would mean more money to educate my children, to see that they have better things in life."

—Ida May Phillips

Phillips lost her case in the lower courts, but never lost her determination. She went to the NAACP, whose Legal Defense Fund helped Phillips take her case to the Supreme Court. The court ruled that equally qualified applicants had to be given employment opportunities irrespective of their gender. Phillips won her case and was hired by Martin-Marietta.

In the mid-1960s and early 1970s, as gender barriers broke down little by little, women went to work in record numbers. More than just the workplace changed. Many couples came to depend on two incomes to make the American dream work.

"They expected to own a house which had telephones and refrigerators and vacuum cleaners and things like that in it. They expected to be able to educate their children, and as that began to be part of the fixture of American society, the double income became a necessity in most households."

—Alice Kessler Harris,
historian

"And that's what Ida May Phillips represented for us: a woman who stood up—who applied for that assembly trainee job and said, 'I should be treated no different from a man. I am qualified, I can do the job, and this society should stop discriminating against me because I have borne children.'"

—Elaine Jones

Despite the number of working women, there were still many rules, laws, and regulations on the books that limited opportunities for women. Even traditional fields like teaching viewed women as second-class citizens.

Jo Carol LaFleur was teaching school in Cleveland, Ohio, when she first experienced discrimination on the job. She was happily married and happily pregnant. Then her principal told her she had to leave the classroom.

"I was just dumbfounded. I had never heard of this mandatory maternity policy that the Cleveland District and most other districts in the country had.

"I was in shock. I said, 'You can't do this to me. I'm teaching here because I want to teach here. I'm a wonderful teacher.'"

—*Jo Carol LaFleur*

The Cleveland School Board ordered Jo Carol LaFleur to leave her teaching position mid-year and not come back until her baby was at least three months old. Mrs. LaFleur had never thought she'd have to choose between work and family. She assumed she could have both. She assumed that decision involved no one but herself and her husband.

"I taught in a very low-income area, the heart of the Cleveland ghetto, and it really was important, I felt, to be a positive role model, to be a married woman who waited until she was in her mid-twenties to have a child, after she was married, after she had a job.

"When I went to complain to my union representative, he said to me, 'Mrs. LaFleur, this is just not a big deal. Just go home, just have the baby.' What a small world he lived in."

—Jo Carol LaFleur

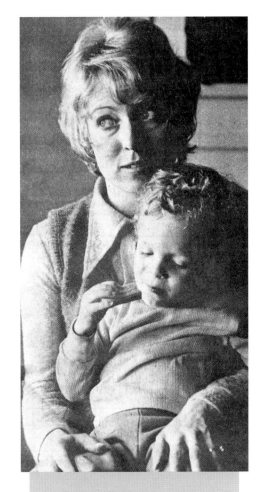

Like Ida May Phillips, Jo Carol LaFleur took her fight to the courtroom.

"At the trial of this matter, the school board defended, using the most ridiculous arguments. Arguments that everybody knows pregnant women have to go to the bathroom all the time; they may not be able to last till the end of class. Arguments that a pregnant woman's center of gravity is so skewed that she may have trouble walking down the hall and maintaining an erect posture. It was so unreasonable."

—Jo Carol LaFleur

The Supreme Court ruled that school boards could not arbitrarily force teachers to give up their jobs during pregnancy, ruling instead that a woman's individual capacity to work should be the determining factor.

Women had won a major victory: the freedom to choose for themselves whether they wanted to work. Jo Carol LaFleur went back to teaching.

"Today, of course, in the nineties, to hear such a tale must seem like it's from Victorian England. It probably is hard to imagine that twenty years ago pregnant women were not permitted to teach. Pregnant women can do anything."

—Jo Carol LaFleur

C. Stephen Babin nor to an association

Jo Carol LaFleur

ersistence changed the law

labels. When I see an in-
I do like to do something

By DAN COOK
me in their Alger Avenue
the young LaFleur family —
and wife, Gordon J. Jr. and Jo
nd their two year old son,
— seem perhaps happier than
milies, but not particularly
al in any other way.

MRS. LAFLEUR, now a teacher at Lakewood High, was the central figure in a lawsuit that has overturned pregnancy leave policies throughout the country after the U.S. Supreme Court ruled in her favor last month.
But the support of her husband and the mere presence of Michael were vital factors in her pursuit of justice all the way to the nation's highest court.
Mrs. LaFleur lost her teaching job in the Cleveland school system in 1971 because she was four months pregnant.
THE SCHOOL'S policy of requiring pregnant teachers to take a leave of absence at that point in their term "just didn't seem fair" to Mrs. LaFleur.
"So I decided to fight it," she said. "It was either that or lose the job."
The Supreme Court ruling, as interpreted by the LaFleurs, strikes down all policies similar to the Cleveland school's former policy, and further demands that institutions treat people "on an individual basis, not as a class."
ONCE YOU start treating people as 'women,' or 'pregnant,' or 'black,' then you know someone is getting the short straw," Mrs. LaFleur said.
The LaFleurs also believe the case can be used as a precedent for

Mrs. LaFleur does not consider herself a crusader or a feminist.
"I HATE labels," she said. "When I see an injustice, I do like to do something about it."
She came to the Cleveland area from her native Richmond, Va. home after she married Gordon, a Fairview Park product.
"I was a social worker when I first came here," she recalled. "I hated it. You can't do anything for people when you're strangled by bureaucracy and red tape."

Title VII had given working women a strong legal tool to assure equal access to jobs, but going case by case through the courts was taking enormous time and money.

The Women's Movement in the 1970s put equality for women on the national agenda. A constitutional amendment guaranteeing equal rights under law was again proposed.

The Equal Rights Amendment had originally been proposed in 1923, right after women won the right to vote. The original architect of the ERA was suffragist Alice Paul. For nearly fifty years, that amendment had been debated and defeated by Congress. Then, in 1972, with the Women's Movement making headlines, Congress passed the ERA. However, it still needed to be ratified by thirty-eight states to become law.

As the ERA went for ratification, women went to their battle stations. Those who supported the ERA were seen as anti-family, while those who opposed the ERA said they were protecting traditional values. It was a battle that seemed to embrace all the conflicts of the twentieth century about the role of women in modern America.

Patricia Schroeder, Congresswoman from Colorado, arrived on Capitol Hill with two small children, just in time to lead the fight for passage of the ERA.

Above: *Suffragist Alice Paul raises a toast to American women.*

"It should have been called the Economic Rights Amendment for Women, because that's really all it was."

—*Patricia Schroeder*

Phyllis Schlafly was a leader among those women opposed to the ERA:

"Most women saw the Equal Rights Amendment as a threat to their status as home-maker and mother, and as a threat to the American family.

"They saw making the financial support laws equal as a threat to the right of a woman to be at home with her baby."

—Phyllis Schlafly

"We were not able to get out to them that the Equal Rights Amendment really helped all women....

"Women, even then, were five times more likely to end up being the sole support of their children than men. That's a pretty astounding statistic that goes right at the Phyllis Schlaflys who think that everybody's being taken care of.

"You know, the seventies people still believed their MRS degree took care of them forever. But your MRS degree didn't take care of very many women."

—Congresswoman Patricia Schroeder
(D) Colorado

"If you took America at the time we started with the ERA—and it's been very slow in evolving since—there were all sorts of jobs where you didn't let women participate.

"You really had a kind of ghettoization of women in the workplace. That's why nursing jobs and teaching jobs have always been the lowest paid—because those were really the only two professions that women could break into. So it really, hardcore, was about economic rights."

—Patricia Schroeder

The ERA was ultimately defeated, three states short of ratification. Today, the fight over the ERA may seem almost irrelevant, as women are working in record numbers and in nearly every kind of job. By the year 2000, eighty percent of American women will be working full- or part-time. The question now isn't "Who will work?" but "Who will do the dishes and change the diapers?" Women, with men, are trying to find the right balance between work and family.

"What needs to change? Men need to change. Men need to begin to understand that work and family are responsibilities of both sexes. Men need to value parenthood as much as they say they value motherhood.

"Children will benefit from having two parents. Men will come to appreciate women's work if they share in it.

"And I'm beginning to see that change; it's not as rapid as some young people would like, but it's certainly better in this generation than it was in the one before."
—Ruth Bader Ginsburg

CHAPTER SIX

First Women

"I've often thought that when something is hard for you, whether it's going to law school or anything else that challenges you, that's probably what you should do. For me, that was making the choice after having fallen in love. I knew how to do well in school. I knew how to start a career. But trying to figure out how to have a relationship with an equal and really to carve that out—that was hard. And I knew that if I walked away from it— if I said to myself, 'Well, there's no opportunity in Arkansas, why should I have to make the choice?'—it would do a great violence to who I was becoming, every day of my life."

—Hillary Rodham Clinton

Edith Wilson

Eleanor Roosevelt

Jacqueline Kennedy

"*I have gotten so interested in reading about all the women who have been in this position. It is like watching the wheel be reinvented. Many of the things that have been said about me have been said many times before about other women, going back into history.*

"*Starting with Martha Washington, whose husband thought she deserved a salary because she had so much work to do as wife of the President, and going through Dolley Madison, who integrated all-male oyster bars and took women to the Congress to watch as the Senators debated the issues. Then moving all the way through history toward our more recent First Ladies, like the second Mrs. Wilson, who kept the country going in many respects, and of course Eleanor Roosevelt.*

"*Mrs. Truman was deeply involved with her husband. Nearly every night they were in the White House together—they would go over his work, she would read his writing, she would critique his speeches. They just didn't choose to let that be publicly known.*

"*Then the women of more recent times speaking out on issues—Jackie Kennedy Onassis single-handedly renovating the White House, or Mrs. Johnson making an incredible mark on our environment, or Mrs. Ford speaking out on breast cancer and ERA when that was not even a subject that was fit for polite company. And looking at what Mrs. Carter did, being the first lady to testify before Congress. I mean you can go and see all the extraordinary talent that these women brought and how every one of them was criticized no matter what she did.*"

—*Hillary Rodham Clinton*

Work or family?—no one has faced this debate more publicly than the women who have occupied the White House. For better or worse, our First Ladies have often defined the way we view women and their roles in society.

The First Lady is often first on the list for criticism and evaluation, especially in terms of her roles as wife and mother. In 1916, Mrs. Edith Wilson was "accused" of running the country during her husband's illness. Eleanor Roosevelt was berated for having her own political agenda. Betty Ford was condemned for speaking out in favor of the ERA. Rosalyn Carter sat in on Cabinet meetings and was regarded as an advisor to her husband.

Betty Ford

However, no First Lady in recent history has encountered the kind of public debate about her role as has Hillary Rodham Clinton, wife of the forty-second president. A lawyer by profession, she has been called a new sort of First Lady—a partner with her husband, an equal.

"I think I always assumed I'd have a job of some kind, and also that I would have kids. And even though I didn't know very many women who had done both, I always assumed I would do both."
—Hillary Rodham Clinton

In doing both, Mrs. Clinton is not unlike millions of her contemporaries. More than fifty percent of American women combine work and family. Yet the emotional debate over whether this is good for society, women, and families continues.

"What we've done is try to impose on women in general some view about what women should or shouldn't do with their lives. There has been a model—where we've tried to make one size fit all—and women have never been the same. And I think we've done violence to women. We did violence to women by telling them in earlier times that they had to stay at home and they had to be primarily committed to their children. We lost millions of artists. We lost judges. We lost doctors. We lost engineers. We lost all kinds of talent. Then we flipped the pendulum as we often do and said, 'OK, now you have to be out in the world.' And we lost good mothers and dedicated community volunteers. Instead, what we have to try to do is say to each woman, 'Live your own life.'"
—Hillary Rodham Clinton

What to keep and what to discard from tradition is an honest debate.

"Women are pulled in many directions at once, and the roads traveled by our mothers may not always be the best indication of how to get to the future."

—*Hillary Rodham Clinton*

"I think my generation kind of stumbled into a lot of this, in part fueled by the aspirations of our mothers. They came out of the depression and the Second World War and went into the homes in suburbia America and devoted themselves to their children. But always with the view that they were doing it so that their children could have more than they had.

"My mother was the best mother anybody could ever have, and I want to be as good a mother to my daughter as she was to me. But she did it differently than I'm doing it. So trying to learn from what she did and take those basic values, but transplant them into my life experience—which is different—I then see how my daughter will move even beyond that.

"But I want there to be continuity, even as she moves into a world of change. I want her to be rooted in the values and ideals of her grandmother. I want her to pick up the experience that I bring from having lived through the sixties and seventies and eighties, and from having confronted a lot of the challenges that we have. But then I think that she and her daughter are going to have such a great opportunity to say 'Here's what I want to do,' and not be so easily moved by others' expectations of them."

—◆—

"I don't think there's any doubt that, for me, motherhood—and particularly my relationship with my daughter—has been one of the best experiences of my life. Watching someone grow and develop— someone who shares some of your views but not all of them, who struggles to find her own independent voice and her own identity— brings up a lot of the same issues that I face.

"I find myself watching and nurturing that process, but like mothers going back thousands of years, wanting to be protective. You know, wanting to say 'Look, you know, life is not always easy. There are a lot of tough spots in the road ahead.' And knowing that in today's world she's not going to leave her father's home and go immediately at the age of fifteen or sixteen or seventeen into the home of her husband where she will begin to produce children—that is not going to be her life pattern. And so she has to be better prepared to deal with issues, even more so than I was."

—*Hillary Rodham Clinton*

"My view of how you live a life is that you try to integrate all of the parts of your life. And I think in many ways women have always understood that. Even when women mostly worked inside the home, they had to balance a lot of demands. I think now it's a more obvious set of juggling demands that you face. But really women have always had to choose between their duties and responsibilities to themselves, to their husbands, to their children, to their fathers, to their mothers, to everybody around them.

"I think that what we've seen happen in the last several decades is that those choices which have always been very personal and struggled through by individual women are now being made at a public level.

"So many things have changed in the last century, but at an accelerated rate in the last thirty or forty years, that it's hard to look back and find your moorings as our grandmothers could do, looking back centuries and saying that their lives in many ways were very much like their ancestors' lives. And that is true not only for women, but also for men. We are charting new ground. And that means there's much more responsibility given to each individual to determine how we will spend our time. And that responsibility can be liberating, but also terribly frightening and burdensome. Because when you have a set, structured life where you know what's expected of you, and everyone around you knows where you fit into the social structure, you don't have to make very many independent decisions.

"Now we're venturing out. And I think that it is hard in the course of a generation to undo the expectations and attitudes of a millennium. And I'm not at all surprised that these debates go on and that the emotions involved are so intense, because they are a part of a new way of living for both men and women."

—Hillary Rodham Clinton

"What we want is a history that takes account of what our lives were like, and which really recognizes the contributions, on the day-to-day level, of both women and men. Then there are going to be a lot of little boys and girls who are going to see role models and are going to understand that women have always made contributions, both at home and in the world outside the home, and that those choices that girls today face—every one of them is legitimate. They should be able to choose what is right for them in their lives, and then watch how their lives unfold."

—Hillary Rodham Clinton

PART TWO

Sexuality & Social Justice

*T*hroughout the twentieth century, women have fought to control their own lives and fashion a system of justice for themselves and all Americans. From contraception and the changing perception of sexuality to basic civil rights, women have confronted social problems, changing the laws to account for all people. The stories of suffrage—the fight of women to gain the right to vote in America—and women's unsung heroism in the Civil Rights Movement are also told in "Sexuality and Social Justice," which brings together the voices of women such as Edna St. Vincent Millay, Margaret Sanger, Gloria Steinem, Eleanor Roosevelt, Alice Paul, and Fannie Lou Hamer.

CHAPTER SEVEN

Kissing & Telling

"More sex, more sexual talk, more sexual jokes, more sexual access, is not necessarily equated with equality for women."

—Estelle Freedman,
historian

"When I talk about sexuality, of course, I'm not just talking about sex. I mean, I'm talking about power relationships between people."

—Paula Giddings,
historian

At the end of the nineteenth century, American women were described as the "gentle sex"—virtuous and chaste. Their role was clear. As both wife and mother, women were expected to be keepers of our country's morality. There were "good women" and "bad women," and everyone knew the difference. But as the twentieth century dawned, the rules began to change.

Previous page: Poet Edna St. Vincent Millay with Eugen Boissevain, 1933.

Going to the movies became one of America's favorite pastimes—ten million went each week—and the motion picture industry began to teach people some of the facts of life.

Life moved at a new tempo—faster, freer, and more daring. Freud's sexual theories reached America, radical Emma Goldman denounced marriage as a form of prostitution, and the pulpit no longer characterized divorce as a one-way ticket to hell. In fact, the country was being bombarded by new ideas that bore little resemblance to the Victorian restraints of the previous generation.

Emma Goldman

"The 'meaning of marriage'—
that was how we referred to sex...."

"My mother was a doctor, and
still she wouldn't tell me anything.
She gave me a book to read and
said that should take care of it."
—responses from the Mosher Survey

Yet despite all the fast talk, many women still suffered from Victorian ignorance about sex. The wedding night could be a rude awakening.

And, as one doctor said in 1902:

"*Too many husbands are ignorant of the sexual needs of their wives. Husbands ought to be taught that the God-given relation is two-sided, and without harmony and mutual enjoyment it becomes mere masturbation to the body and mind of the one who alone is gratified.*"

In 1892, Dr. Clelia Mosher began asking women questions about their sexuality, and she continued her forthright surveys into the new century. Her motivation was simple:

"The satisfaction beyond all others of work which will bring a larger measure of life and useful-ness to other human beings—a sense of helping woman...back to her high estate of equal partner in life."
—Clelia Mosher

Mosher surveyed married, educated women. But the sexual-ly explicit findings, which would have shocked the public, were never published. The survey, hidden among her personal papers, was only discovered by accident in 1974. The Mosher Survey, believed to be the first of its kind ever solicited in America, gives us an unprece-dented view into the post-Victorian bedroom.

"The findings in this survey suggested that, in marriage, these women felt that sex was impor-tant, and that they certainly had the capacity for enjoying sexual relations. Many of them expressed great interest and great pleasure in having orgasmic sexual rela-tions with their husbands...."
—Estelle Freedman

Dr. Clelia Mosher

Mosher's survey asked, "Is intercourse agreeable to you or not?"

Many of the women answering the survey were pleased with their sexual experiences:

"I believe reasonable intercourse conduces health, and I am sure it makes married life the happiest state in the world on account of the spiritual union that results from it."

Other wives were not so lucky:

"I ran away after one month, but was sent back by my parents and told to behave. I know intercourse is necessary to keep the home together and keep the man satisfied."

Clelia Mosher never married. She put herself through the Johns Hopkins Medical School and devoted her life to studying female physiology. She used the knowledge she gained to publish books for women. She wrote honestly about subjects such as menstruation and menopause, challenging prevailing notions about feminine fragility.

Mosher published *Health and the Woman Movement* in 1915, *Women's Physical Freedom* in 1923, and *Personal Hygiene for Women* in 1927. While modest about the books themselves, she felt strongly about their goals—to educate women:

"This little book does not attempt to cover the whole field of personal hygiene, but deals only with some of the special problems of women's health, concerning which the lack of knowledge has been so disastrous to women...."

Mosher became an Associate Professor of Personal Hygiene and medical advisor to women at Stanford University. Her desire to speak honestly about sexual matters was put to the test by these students, who often sought answers to some disturbingly frank questions—questions they dared not ask their own mothers.

"The lectures on personal hygiene are exhausting me more than they should. Where should I draw the line? My Victorian sense of decent reticence is constantly shocked. These girls should have any question they ask answered honestly and sanely. The shock is that they should be able to ask without hesitation in class. Is it that these things of sex are purely academic questions? I think where there is so much smoke, there must be some fire. It is a new age, new thinking, new ideas; or does it mean no ideals?"

—Clelia Mosher

Mosher was right—there was fire. In the first decades of the new century, young women left home in record numbers to go to work. Relations between men and women would never be the same again.

"When women go into factories, when women go eventually into offices, they work alongside of men, they get to know each other socially. After work, you might have men and women going out and socializing in much less chaperoned ways than they had in an earlier culture where courtship took place within the family setting."
—Estelle Freedman

World War I further accelerated change. The war catapulted women into the public world. They went to work in defense plants, took over family finances, and spoke out on issues. In 1920, women won the vote, much to the dismay of many Americans who wanted to keep women away from the sordid business of politics.

But one of the most shocking changes was the birth of the "Jazz Baby," the daughters of the women who had discreetly answered Dr. Clelia Mosher's sex survey. It seemed as if, in just one generation, women had gone from demure to daring.

Right: *Dramatic actress Theda Bara.* **Opposite page:** *Edna St. Vincent Millay.*

Poet Edna St. Vincent Millay epitomized the Jazz Age. She publicly flaunted her many lovers and lived her life as if it were one long, passionate spree. She was quoted, copied, imitated, and satirized. Her comings and goings were reported on in gossip columns as if she were a movie star. Young women saw Millay as someone to emulate, much to the dismay of their parents.

"Everyone who was alive during that time remembers how rapidly customs, manners, and ideas in American life altered during the decade of careless wealth, crumbling standards, and deliberate revolt against society. Edna's flippant lines were the Marseillaise of that particular revolution."
—Vincent Sheehan, journalist

Millay's poems were a constant assault on conventional morality—they questioned marriage, championed brutal honesty between lovers, and cast a clear eye on love. The public couldn't get enough of her romantic despair.

"She had an intoxicating effect on people. It was impossible not to fall in love with her. There was something of awful drama about everything one did with Edna."
—Edmund Wilson, literary critic

"And if I loved you Wednesday,

Well, what is that to you?

I do not love you Thursday—

So much is true.

And why you come complaining

Is more than I can see.

I loved you Wednesday,—yes—but what

Is that to me?"

—Edna St. Vincent Millay,
"Thursday"

"I shall forget you presently, my dear,

So make the most of this, your little day,

Your little month, your little half a year...."

—Edna St. Vincent Millay,
Sonnet XI

Millay's parents divorced when she was young. Edna, who preferred to be called by her middle name, Vincent, grew up in Maine spending considerable time taking care of her two younger sisters. Her mother, a nurse, earned money to support the family.

Millay's first poem, "Renascence," was published in 1912, when she was only twenty years old. In 1913, she was accepted to Vassar, an all-women's college in upstate New York. At Vassar, Millay's first romantic involvements were with women.

"Millay was a creature of the nineteenth-century Victorian culture where men and women occupied very separate spheres. Institutions like Vassar were all women—faculty and students. Then, in a funny way, a world where sexuality was more repressed, where men and women were separate, allowed for more diversity of sexual experience.... Millay seems to have spent her life comfortable sexually with men and women."

—Ellen Chesler,
historian

After graduating from Vassar in 1917, Millay moved to Greenwich Village. The Village was a gathering place for radicals and artists who scoffed at conventional ideas. For these free-thinkers, passion and marriage had little to do with one another. There Millay met Floyd Dell, a writer and political activist who would become her first male lover.

"There began for us a romance that was haunted by her sense of the inevitable impermanence of love. She refused to marry me. We parted—several times. She fell in love with other men and then came back to me. We always forgave each other the hurt of love."

—Floyd Dell

Like the careless heroines of F. Scott Fitzgerald's novels, like the daring flappers in the movies, Millay embodied the reckless desperation of the twenties. And American youths loved her for it. Her collections of poetry often reached the top of the bestseller lists, and in 1923, she became the first woman to win the Pulitzer Prize for poetry.

In 1923, Millay married Eugen Boissevain, a coffee exporter and ardent supporter of women's rights. Her marriage shocked many of her friends, who believed that she would spend her entire life going from one lover to another.

"She, to whom freedom is a religion, submitted to the matrimonial yoke. Greenwich Village had predicted that she would never marry, that she was too fond of freedom, that she would choose single blessedness in preference to the slavery of marriage."
—The New York Times, *19 July 1923*

But poor health took its toll on Millay, who had burned her candle at both ends through most of her life. She suffered a nervous breakdown in the mid-forties, and although she continued to write and often championed political causes, her flamboyance was gone. She died on October 19, 1950.

"What lips my lips have kissed, and where, and why,

I have forgotten, and what arms have lain

Under my head till morning; but the rain

Is full of ghosts tonight, that tap and sigh

Upon the glass and listen for reply,

And in my heart there stirs a quiet pain

For unremembered lads that not again

Will turn to me at midnight with a cry...."

—Edna St. Vincent Millay,
from Sonnet XLII

*Top: Millay and husband Eugen Boissevain aboard ship on their 1924 around-the-world tour. **Opposite page, top:** Millay in her teens. **Opposite page, middle:** Millay, at Vassar, with a friend.*

Hard times were on the horizon. The easy money and free-wheeling sexuality of the Jazz Age were no match for the bitter reality of the coming Depression.

Sexual outrageousness was losing its public luster. The transformation came not a moment too soon for writer Charlotte Perkins Gilman, who spoke for many moralists when she criticized pleasure seekers like Millay.

"This newly liberated woman is, underneath it all, shallow and self-indulgent. It's simple appetite and impulse, coarseness and looseness of speech, dress and habit of life. Women are made to be mothers, and not, as seems widely supposed, for enjoyable preliminaries."

—Charlotte Perkins Gilman

Margaret Sanger, a nurse working with immigrants in New York, would devote her life to proving Gilman wrong. Sanger believed women certainly should be mothers if they so chose, but she also knew firsthand that women were definitely "made for enjoyable preliminaries."

Top: Charlotte Perkins Gilman, 1915
Right: Margaret Sanger

CHAPTER EIGHT

The Woman Rebel

"Margaret Sanger's real pro-found contribution to her time and our own was in changing public discourse. Not only about contra-ception, but about sexuality. It wasn't as though there was no contraception around, but nobody talked about it in public. She insist-ed on bringing it out into the public, and that's a very important distinction."

—Ellen Chesler,
historian

y advice for women who do not want children—get a divorce and vacate the position for some other woman who is able and willing to fulfill all a wife's duties as well as to enjoy her privileges."

—*"Sexual Hygiene" pamphlet, 1902*

The "privilege" of childbirth took the lives of three hundred thousand women between the years of 1910 and 1925. That's more than all the men who died in American wars from the Revolution until World War I. Women were desperate for a way out of constant pregnancies. They found a champion in Margaret Sanger.

"My husband is afraid I will use something which will injure me, but I tell him I'd rather be dead than have another wee one, no matter how much I love them. Please, Mrs. Sanger, help me...."

"I am the mother of three. I would rather die than have another as we can't do what we ought for the three we have."

"I have ten living children. The doctor says if I had any more I won't live through it, but he will not tell me what to do to prevent me getting any more."

"I am sixteen years old and married and have two children. I married a poor man and I don't want to bring any more children into poverty."

"Mrs. Sanger, I am the mother of six children. After the birth of a child I go insane for about four months. The doctor says I should stop having children, but he won't tell me how. Will you please help me?"

"All children should be wanted and loved. That's the goal of everything I do."

—Margaret Sanger

Top: *Mrs. Shotbag, a woman who delivered all four of her children herself, Williston, North Carolina, 1937.* **Opposite page, top left:** *Margaret Sanger.*

"The biggest mistake women make is keeping their mouths shut and their wombs open."
—Emma Goldman,
political activist

Above: *Emma Goldman* **Below:** *Margaret Sanger conversing with other women.*

"If women are ever going to have a satisfactory sex life, we have to get control over reproduction. Having a baby every time we sleep with our husband is literally killing women before their time."
—Margaret Sanger

In 1910, Margaret Sanger, a trained nurse, moved with her husband and three children to New York City. There she met the freethinkers who would change her life. One of her early influences was Emma Goldman, an outspoken advocate of reproductive freedom and women's rights.

Margaret Sanger—along with Goldman and other audacious women such as Crystal Eastman and Mary Ware Dennett—first brought the issues of family limitation to the public. Sanger would devote her life to the cause of reproductive freedom. It was she who coined the phrase *Birth Control.*

"Well, it was my grandmother's major focus her entire life. Her mother had died at the age of forty-seven, eighteen pregnancies, eleven living children. My grandmother felt that if women were ever going to contribute to society in any remarkable way, they had to have control over the number of children that they bore, and then be able to provide their children with an environment where they could grow to be healthy and productive citizens."
—Margaret Lampe,
granddaughter of Margaret Sanger

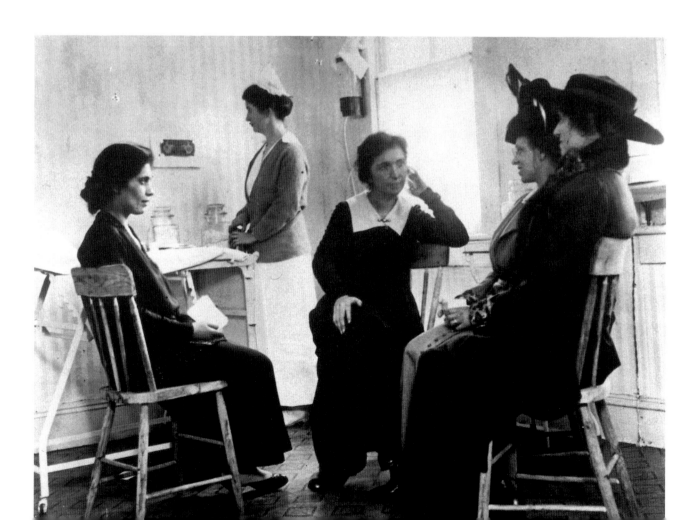

Some forms of birth control were available, but many women still didn't know what contraceptives were, or how to get them. As pharmacist said in 1912,

"It was easy to purchase a kind of diaphragm from any pharmacy. It was the Mizpah pessary and we sold it as a womb support for a distended uterus, which was a common condition usually caused by too many pregnancies. And of course doctors could prescribe condoms, but they were given out to prevent venereal disease, not to prevent pregnancy."

"There was a great deal of hypocrisy in this time because in fact birth rates had begun to decline among the middle classes. But poor women and immigrant women, particularly, who didn't know the culture or know the language, were disadvantaged by the fact that there was no public knowledge or public discussion of the availability of contraception."

—Ellen Chesler

"I heard over and over again of their desperate efforts at 'bringing themselves around'—steaming over a chamber of boiling coffee or of turpentine water, rolling down stairs, inserting knitting needles or shoe hooks into the uterus."

—Margaret Sanger

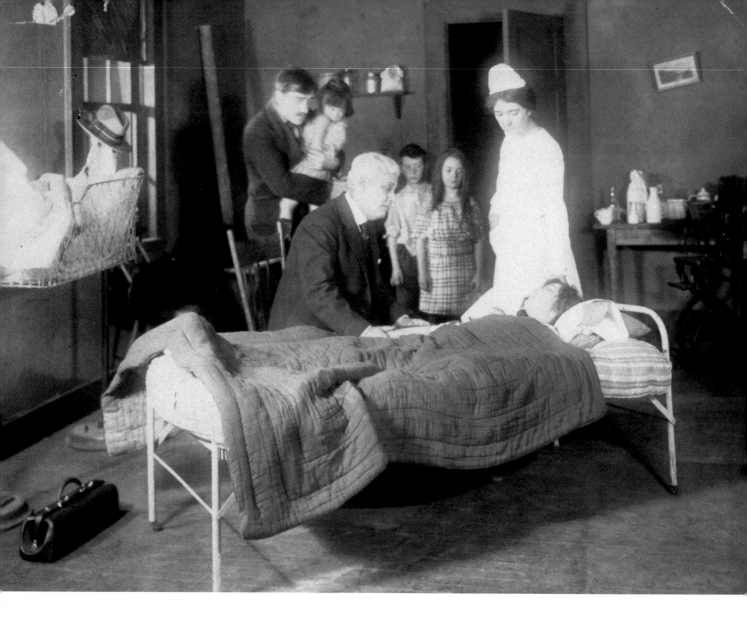

While her husband, William, pursued his ambitions as an artist and architect, Sanger helped support the family as a nurse. It was 1912.

"I worked on the Lower East Side of New York. What I saw there was horrible. I'll never forget Sadie. She had four babies, one after another. I nursed her back from death's door with each one. The doctor told her her body had just given out from pregnancies. Sadie begged me to tell her the secret rich women had for not getting pregnant. She asked the doctor what to do and he just said, 'Tell Jake to sleep on the roof.'

"Well, he didn't, and within a year Sadie was pregnant again and dying. Watching this young woman die from nothing more than having too many babies, I made the decision that night to do whatever I could to give women more control over their bodies."

—Margaret Sanger

Above: *Sanger at the bedside of a sick patient.* **Opposite page, top:** *William Sanger* **Opposite page, center:** *First edition of* The Woman Rebel, *Margaret Sanger's monthly newspaper, 1914.*

"Suddenly my wife was transformed. She devoured every article and book she could lay her capable hands on—she attended meetings and lectures and plunged into welfare work. Gone forever was the conservative Irish girl I had married—a new woman, forceful, intelligent, hungry for facts, tireless, ambitious, and cool, had miraculously come into being."

—William Sanger

In 1914, in clear defiance of the Comstock anti-obscenity laws which gave the Post Office jurisdiction over deciding what could be termed pornography, Sanger published her own monthly newspaper, *The Woman Rebel*.

THE WOMAN REBEL
NO GODS NO MASTERS

VOL I. MARCH 1914 NO. 1.

THE AIM

his paper will not be the champion of any "ism."

... rebel women are invited to contribute to its columns.

... majority of papers usually address themselves to the ideas of their ... but the WOMAN REBEL will ... tely refuse to be adjusted.

... aim of this paper will be to stimulate working women to think for themselves and to build up a conscious ... character.

... rly feature will be a series of ... written by the editor for girls ... rteen to eighteen years of age. ... esent chaos of sex atmosphere ... ult for the girl of this uncer... to know just what to do or ... at constitutes clean living ... rudishness. All this slushy ... white slavery, the man paint... cribed as a hideous vulture ... own upon the young, pure ... girl, drugging her through ... of grape juice and lemon... n dragging her off to his ... other men equally as vi... nd fatten on her enforced ... ely this picture is enough ... disgust every thinking ... n, who has lived even a ... t the adolescent age, ... repulsive and foul con... be given to adolescent ... ation for life than this ... being perpetuated by ... orant in the name of

was with a sweetheart or through the desire for a sweetheart or something impelling within themselves, the nature of which they knew not, neither could they control. Society does not forgive this act when it is based upon the natural impulses and feelings of a young girl. It prefers the other story of the grape juice procurer which makes it easy to shift the blame from its own shoulders, to cast the stone and to evade the unpleasant facts that it alone is responsible for. It sheds sympathetic tears over white slavery, holds the often mythical procurer up as a target, while in reality it is supported by the misery it engenders.

If, as reported, there are approximately 35,000 women working as prostitutes in New York City alone, is it not sane to conclude that some force, some living, powerful, social force is at play to compel these women to work at a trade which involves police persecution, social ostracism and the constant danger of exposure to venereal diseases. From my own knowledge of adolescent girls and from sincere expressions of women working as prostitutes inspired by mutual understanding and confidence I claim that the first sexual act of these so-called wayward girls is partly given, partly desired yet reluctantly so because of the fear of the consequences together with the dread of lost respect of the man. These fears interfere with mutuali...

lows." His sole aim is to throw off responsibility. The same uncertainty in these emotions is experienced by girls in marriage in as great a proportion as in the unmarried. After the first experience the life of a girl varies. All these girls do not necessarily go into prostitution. They have had an experience which has not "ruined" them, but rather given them a larger vision of life, stronger feelings and a broader understanding of human nature. The adolescent girl does not understand herself. She is full of contradictions, whims, emotions. For her emotional nature longs for caresses, to touch, to kiss. She is often as well satisfied to hold hands or to go arm in arm with a girl as in the companionship of a boy.

It is these and kindred facts upon which the WOMAN REBEL will dwell from time to time and from which it is hoped the young girl will derive some knowledge of her nature, and conduct her life upon such knowledge.

It will also be the aim of the WOMAN REBEL to advocate the prevention of conception and to impart such knowledge in the columns of this paper.

Other subjects, including the slavery through motherhood; through things, the home, public opinion and so forth, will be dealt with.

It is also the aim of this paper to circulate among those women who work in prostitution; to voice their wrongs; to expose the police persecution which hovers over them and to give free expression to their thoughts, hopes and opinions.

And at all times the WOMAN REBEL will strenuously advocate economic emancipation.

THE NEW FEMINISTS

That apologetic tone of the new American feminists which plainly says "Really, Madam Public Opinion, we are all quite harmless and perfectly respectable" was the keynote of the first and second mass meetings held at Cooper Union on the 17th and 20th of February last.

The ideas advanced were very old and time-worn even to the ordinary church-going woman who reads the magazines and comes in contact with current thought. The "right to ignore fashions," the "right to work," "right to keep her own name," the "right to organize," the "right of the mother to work"; all these so-called rights fail to arouse enthusiasm because to-day they are all recognized by society and there...

"A woman's duty is to look the whole world in the face with a go to hell look in the eyes, to have an ideal, to speak and act in defiance of convention."

—Margaret Sanger

The bold, informative paper, which gave information on such taboo subjects as menstruation and female physiology, was censored and Margaret Sanger was indicted. To avoid jail, she used a counterfeit passport and fled to Europe, leaving behind her two sons and her young daughter, Peggy.

"Dear Peggy, how my heart goes out to you. I could weep from loneliness for you— just to touch your soft chubby hands—but work is to be done, dear—work to make your path easier—and those who come after you."

While Sanger was in Europe, attention was focused on another birth control crusader, Mary Ware Dennett. Dennett, who came from a prominent Boston family noted for its social reformers, formed the National Birth Control League to fight for legal reform. When she took her cause to Congress, her arguments were greeted with derision.

"I believe that everyone who was born was born because of an accident, and not because they were wanted. I feel that if the law is amended, it would permit women to have more lapdogs and encourage the idle to be more idle."
—James Watson,
Senator from Indiana

"You cannot cheat nature. I do not think it should be left to the whim of women to decide whether she shall have children or not."
—W. H. McMaster,
Senator from South Dakota

Top: Margaret Sanger with her two sons. Center: Senator James Watson

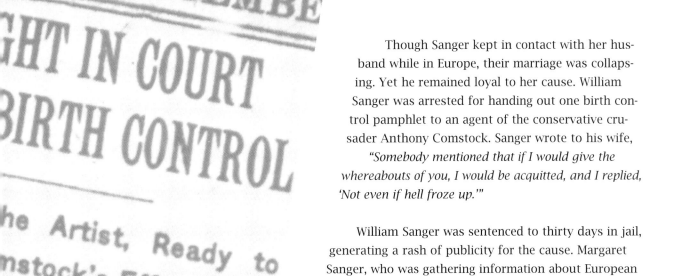

EMBE
GHT IN COURT
BIRTH CONTROL

he Artist, Ready to
mstock's Efforts to
ess Discussion.

A HUMAN RIGHT

rdships to Parents
en Through III-
d Families.

nger, artist and archi-
leventh Street, comes
Special Sessions on
d to a charge of cir-
literature, his case
he interest of those
discussion of birth
rested in January,
t in two courts for
has lost, and yes-
hat he will plead
ght to trial.
Mr. Sanger is ac-
one on "Family
his wife, Mar-
a trained nurse
and worked for
to control birth.
where she has

Though Sanger kept in contact with her husband while in Europe, their marriage was collaps-
ing. Yet he remained loyal to her cause. William
Sanger was arrested for handing out one birth control pamphlet to an agent of the conservative crusader Anthony Comstock. Sanger wrote to his wife,
*"Somebody mentioned that if I would give the
whereabouts of you, I would be acquitted, and I replied,
'Not even if hell froze up.'"*

William Sanger was sentenced to thirty days in jail,
generating a rash of publicity for the cause. Margaret
Sanger, who was gathering information about European
birth control methods, decided that the time was right
to return home and face her own trial.

However, a greater crisis awaited her. A few days
after her return, Sanger's daughter,
Peggy, was taken ill with pneumo-
nia.

*"Peggy died the morning
of November 6, 1915.... The joy
in the fullness of life went out
of it then and has never quite
returned."*
—Margaret Sanger

*"I don't think that my
grandmother ever forgave herself for the death of her daughter. She used to say to us 'There
is nothing more devastating than
losing a child.'"*
—Margaret Lampe

In an unusual display of sen-
sitivity, the judge offered Sanger
a postponement of her trial. She
refused and went to court.

The charges of publishing
obscene material were dropped.
Sanger mustered her strength and continued her
fight.

In Europe, Sanger had seen clinics that dispensed information and birth control devices to women. She had a vision of birth control clinics across the United States. Forty-six Amboy Street in the Brownsville section of Brooklyn became the site of America's first family planning clinic.

"No doctors would help us. My sister Ethel, a nurse, and I talked to the women. All we could do was provide contraceptive information and sex education. We couldn't, by law, dispense condoms or fit diaphragms. We charged only ten cents for each consultation.

"All the women who came seeking information were workingmen's wives. All had children. No unmarried girls came at all."
—Margaret Sanger

"I toured the country meeting Society Club women and social workers, always hearing the nonsense of confusing contraception with abortion. And always, behind every question, was the desire to know the safest method for limiting families."
—Margaret Sanger

After only nine days, police raided the clinic. Margaret, Ethel, and another woman who worked at the clinic were arrested and charged with violations of the obscenity laws.

"My sister went to jail first and went on a hunger strike. This act gained us national attention. Ethel won a pardon and I went to jail, this time for thirty days. While in jail I read to the women there—mostly illiterate drug addicts and prostitutes. I talked to them about birth control and sex education—they were appallingly ignorant. Finally the matron told me to stop—she said the women were bad enough already."

—Margaret Sanger

"Her jail sentence in 1917 in New York had won a reinterpretation of New York law that allowed for doctors to prescribe birth controls. She opened up clinics and went to the physicians of this country with her message because of that."

—Ellen Chesler

Sanger continued to travel the country and the world, championing the cause of birth control. It was still illegal to import contraceptives, but that didn't stop Margaret Sanger.

*Above: Margaret Sanger and her sister Ethel, together in court. **Opposite page, top:** Carriages lined up outside Sanger's family planning clinic. **Opposite page, bottom:** The Sanger Clinic Research Bureau, Manhattan, 1923.*

89

"On her trip to France she met a man who owned a brandy distillery company. She said, 'Ah ha!' I will see if the man who owns the brandy distillery will take the diaphragms and ship them for me. So they took brandy bottles and stuffed them with diaphragms, crated them up, and marked those crates with X's. They went on the ship, and off they went to the United States.

"The captain of the boat was told that when he entered the harbor, he was to put the black 'X' boxes overboard to float in the water. She knew a man who delivered coal in their apartment building, and she enlisted Vito's help. He had a tugboat. He was also the father of fourteen children. And that made him very interested in this cause. She asked him if he would help her smuggle those contraceptives into this country.

"He said on one condition—that his wife would get one of the devices. And so, at two in the morning, my grandmother and Vito went out in the tugboat and retrieved these crates that were floating, because of course they were very light. They dragged them into shore, where women were waiting with empty suitcases to accept the brandy bottles. And this is the way the first diaphragm entered the United States."
—Margaret Lampe & Nancy Pallesen,
granddaughters of Margaret Sanger

"Margaret remarried in 1921, after her divorce from William Sanger, to a millionaire, Jay Noah Slee. He bankrolled the birth control movement and supported her cause. She turned her back on the radicalism of her past, but I would say she didn't change her end so much as her means. She figured out that she could continue to promote her cause, but not by opposing the establishment, by working with it."
—Ellen Chesler

Right: Volunteers sell Birth Control Review.
Opposite page: Margaret Sanger

WALLACE: "When Mrs. Margaret Sanger opened the first birth control clinic in the United States back in 1916, birth control was a dirty word.

"Today your opposition stems mainly from where, from what source?"

SANGER: "Well, I think the opposition is mainly from the hierarchy of the Roman Catholic Church."

WALLACE: "You certainly can take no issue with the natural law as the hierarchy of the Catholic Church regards it."

SANGER: "Well, I certainly do take issue with it, and I think it's untrue, and I think it's unnatural. Nothing bears it out because it's an unnatural attitude to take. And how do they know? I mean, after all, they're celibates—they don't know love, they don't know marriage. They know nothing about bringing up children or any of the marriage problems of life. And yet, they speak to people as if they were God.

"My feeling is that love, and the attraction between men and women—in many cases the very finest relationship—has nothing to do with bearing a child. It's secondary. Many, many times, you see your birth rate, and you talk to people who have very happy marriages and they're not having babies every year. Yes, I think that's a celibate attitude. Surely."

Even as late as the 1950s, Margaret Sanger—now in her seventies—was defending the idea and practice of birth control.

"I was playing devil's advocate—I would take a considered position to raise questions so that the audience would think about things that they might not have been comfortable thinking about, or that they wanted to think about but didn't want to enunciate. So we were a surrogate, to ask some of the questions about feminism, about birth control, about the relationships of men and women back then.

"It was groundbreaking. It sounds so pedestrian, so ordinary, today in '93. But in 1957, this was revolution. Women didn't talk that way...in public."

—Mike Wallace, 1994

People may not have been talking about it, but attitudes were definitely changing. Margaret Sanger's ideas would be the seeds of a revolution.

NATION

Female condoms headed for stores th

ASSOCIATED PRESS

Washington — Female condoms will start appearing in American drugstores this summer after the Food and Drug Administration acted Thursday to allow an American company to ship them into the country.

The FDA notified Wisconsin Pharmacal, which makes the Reality female condom, that it had approved the company's importing the condoms from their manufacturing plant in London, said company spokeswoman Holly Birnbaum Sherman.

The Reality female condom was ap-

proved by the FDA in May 1993. It is currently available only at some family planning clinics and AIDS treatment centers, mostly on the East and West coasts.

It will retail for about $2.50 per condom, packaged three to a box, wrapped and prelubricated in individual packets, with additional lubricant provided.

The Reality condom will be available in August, Sherman said.

Sherman said while Reality acts as a contraceptive, it is designed to reduce the risk of sexually transmitted diseases. The con-

dom, made of thane, covers canal and pa

Women u searchers th condom and hours befor

But one some wome dom is a cy ible rings protrudes

CHAPTER NINE

Miniskirts Are Not A Revolution

"The fifties were the most desperate decade. We wore merry widows to cinch in our waists and we wore girdles and we wore impossibly structured bras, and everybody was supposed to, in spite of all this selling of sex, remain virginal. There was a very high price on being a virgin when you married."

—*Gloria Steinem,
author*

oys will be boys, but girls should remain pure. That's the age-old double standard which, in the 1950s, reached new heights of hypocrisy. Music, television, and movies all mirrored the mixed message.

There was also a high value placed on motherhood. During the fifties, the country's birth rate increased for the first time in more than a hundred years, resulting in the twentieth century's only baby boom. Movies made for high school girls encouraged them to welcome pregnancy—after marriage, of course.

But at the same time, efforts to find an effective means of birth control also increased. The research was funded in large part by a woman—Katherine McCormick—heir to the vast International Harvester fortune. Like her good friend Margaret Sanger, McCormick devoted her life and many millions of dollars to the pursuit of a simple means of birth control. In 1960, their goal was realized when the FDA approved use of the Birth Control Pill.

Overnight, it seemed, America had an effective, easy to use, widely available means of birth control. Moralists feared sexual restraint had just been delivered a death blow. The implications of sex without procreation were terrifying.

Time magazine grappled with America's fears:

"Does the convenient contraceptive promote promiscuity? In some cases, no doubt it does—as did the automobile, the drive-in movie, and the motel. But the consensus among both physicians and sociologists is that a girl who is promiscuous on the pill would have been promiscuous without it."

"The pill is very important in becoming the new favorite form of birth control within marriage. And it is also very important in causing women to rethink sexual behavior when the expectation that if you're on the pill you're available begins to circulate, particularly in the youth culture."

—Estelle Freedman,
historian

The 1960s brought a series of social upheavals that redefined women's roles, culminating in the radical idea that sexuality and reproduction were no longer synonymous. The media crowned it "The Sexual Revolution," and women were as eager as men to storm the barricades.

"Not being a raving beauty, I thought, 'Wow, there's a lot of guys here. You know, they're more interested in me than I thought.' So it sort of added to self-esteem to have these things happen on a sort of continuing basis. And I know that sounds flippant, but, I mean, I was young and I was flippant. And, yeah, I enjoyed it."

—Grace Slick,
singer

Baby Boomers were now in their twenties, and casting off their parents' antiquated ideas—including the value of virginity—was a rite of passage. In the sixties, it was politics, not sex, that mattered.

"Morality has to do with the Vietnam war, whether or not the House Unamerican Activities Committee is functioning properly, whether or not there is racial discrimination in any part of our country. These are moral questions to today's students. The question of whether or not a young man sleeps with his girlfriend isn't perceived as a moral issue."

—Professor John Manning,
University of Michigan, 1967

"I think it was probably my ex who made up the title 'Girls Say Yes to Boys Who Say No.' At the time he was still using the word chick *in his speeches, and running into some very serious problems from the audience.*

"We thought it was really a pro-draft resistance poster, and the proceeds went to draft resistance, and I thought it was, you know, ultra-revolutionary. Then I was visited by local women from the Women's Liberation Movement. And they were absolutely furious with me. I literally did not know what they were talking about. I mean, I was out to lunch on the topic. I was newly married, I was pregnant, I was running around the kitchen making cookies for them and bringing them tea. And they were sitting and fuming on my couch, wanting to talk about the issue of this poster. I mean, 'girls,' number one, you don't use that word. We have no business saying 'yes' to guys for anything. It was flying right over my head. I really didn't know what they were talking about until, I think, probably several years later, when I began piecing it together."

—Joan Baez,
singer

"I think you can see their criticisms in the early Feminist Movement or the Women's Liberation Movement of the 1970s, saying the sexual revolution is for men. It's giving men more access to women, but it may not be in women's interest or for women."

—Estelle Freedman

As it turned out, the "Summer of Love" lasted only a few short seasons. Sexual fun and games were cut short as women began to question whether being a "hippie chick" was really *liberation*.

Erica Jong became a spokesperson for the sexual revolution with the publication of *Fear of Flying*. Jong pronounced the double standard dead and celebrated female sexuality. The unabashed adventures of her heroine delighted and shocked Jong's many readers.

"I was just chronicling what people were saying to themselves in their heads. And the outrage was amazing. And yet, people were reading the book and passing it from hand to hand and saying, 'Read this, it's the story of my life.'"

—Erica Jong

"In the Hite Report, you can
see echoes of Clelia Mosher's
patients. You can see women who
embrace sexuality as something
that they enjoy, but who are also
very troubled by the double standard, and who feel that they may
not want sex in the same context
as men."

—Estelle Freedman

In the seventies, women were talking frankly with one another as never before. Everything was out in the open—nothing was
private, little was taboo. Surveys about sex were commonplace,
as Americans tried to discover how women regarded their new-
found sexual freedom. None of these surveys was more frank
than the *Hite Report.*

*"I decided to do a questionnaire on sexuality because we were
talking about it, and it seemed like it must be part of the overall
'oppression of women.' And so everyone said, 'Oh, that's a good
idea. Go and do that.' So I asked women essay questions about
'well, when do you have orgasms?' And, 'how do you have
orgasms?' And, 'how do you feel about it?'"*

—*Shere Hite,*
author of the Hite Report

Women responded to Hite's inquiries in record numbers.
Their answer was that sex in an age of sexual freedom wasn't
always bliss.

"Even today, there are a lot of women who are very frightened of sex and afraid that they're going to be labeled 'slut.' When I walk into my daughter's room and she's labeling a girl a slut with her friends, I give them such a lecture. I say, 'you are not allowed to call another woman a slut just because she enjoys her sexuality.' Well, that's very strong stuff coming from Mom, but what's underneath it is the judging of women that constantly goes on. We don't want to continue that judging."

—Erica Jong

"In the Hite Report, I was constantly referring to patriarchal culture and saying that you can have a different culture, we can make a different culture. It doesn't leave men out. But it certainly doesn't put women in second place anymore. And this is what we're moving toward. This is what we're doing. Sex is just part of it."

—Shere Hite

*"Economic equality and political equality
have to take place to make sexual equality possible.
If women can't afford birth control, if women don't have
access to abortion, if women don't have access to equal
salaries, or to an impact on public policy, simply being more
available for sex is not going to free women."*
—Estelle Freedman

*"Sexual freedom in itself does not bring happiness. It
seems to me that women don't want sex that has no tenderness
or commitment with it. Sometimes they just want to have fun,
but usually, at a point in a woman's life she reaches a level
of maturity really, where she just doesn't want to do it on
the road with any Hell's Angel."*
—Erica Jong

CHAPTER TEN

The March To The Ballot Box

"The vote was just as important to women symbolically as it was in terms of what they would do with it politically. Many of these women were now college trained, they were very involved in their communities, and to them it was a slap in the face that their husbands could vote, and they could not. They felt they were citizens, they felt they were participating. And why was it that they couldn't go to the ballot box once a year, or once every four years, and vote?"

—Susan Ware,
historian

INEZ MILHOLLAND BOISSEVAIN

WHO DIED FOR THE FREEDOM of WOMEN.

*S*eptember, 1916. A beautiful, young woman named Inez Milholland toured the country, campaigning relentlessly for the right of American women to vote. She pleaded with President Wilson to support woman's suffrage.

One day, exhausted from her labors and her health depleted by pernicious anemia, Milholland collapsed. She was rushed to a hospital and, despite heroic efforts by her doctors, died within weeks. She was only thirty years old.

Suffrage had its first martyr. The battle over votes for women—often treated as a joke in the press—turned deadly serious.

But support for *universal* suffrage—the right of all people to vote regardless of race, class, education, or sex—was splintered even among women.

One group of suffragists—the National American Woman Suffrage Association, led by Carrie Chapman Catt—made a case for taking the vote away from illiterate men and giving it to educated women.

"The government is menaced with great danger. That danger lies in the votes possessed by males in the slums of the cities. There is but one way to avert the danger. Cut off the vote to the slums and give it to women."

—Carrie Chapman Catt,
suffragist

"The situation is dangerous. We often hear the remark nowadays that women will get the vote if they try hard enough and persistently. And it is true that they will get it and play havoc with it for themselves and society, if men are not firm enough and wise enough and—it must be said—masculine enough to prevent them."

—The New York Times,
1912

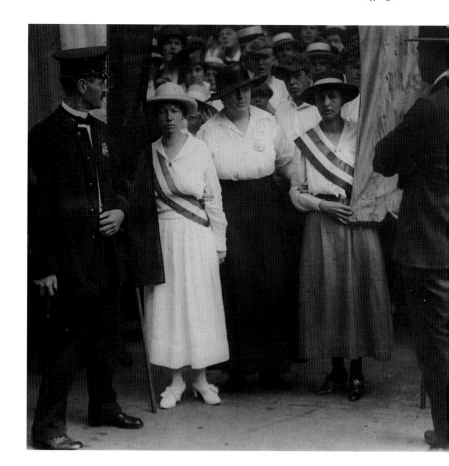

The fight for the vote also divided white and black women.

"The National Association of Colored Women is concerned most that women shall have the vote, and that the word 'women' shall include colored women without question or equivocation."
—Elizabeth C. Carter,
suffragist

Even Alice Paul—who led the National Woman's Party, which fought for suffrage at the national level—was willing to let political expediency undermine justice for black women:
"We are organizing white women in the South; we have heard of no activity among the Negresses."

Paul was playing politics. She knew very well that black women wanted the vote, but she believed the South needed to be appeased if the Nineteenth Amendment—Suffrage—was to be ratified.

"A lot of people were nervous about what seemed to be a challenge to traditional gender roles. The view was that women should be at home, and they should define themselves as wives and mothers. Letting them vote was confirmation that they had roles outside of the family. And to many people, at a time of enormous change, this was very threatening."
—Susan Ware

"People said that if you give black women the vote, that's going to be the end of white supremacy in the South. Well, this is, I mean in all fairness, quite a problem to predominantly white women's organizations who needed southern votes in order to get the amendment passed to get women's suffrage."
—Paula Giddings,
historian

Above: Women attending college conference.
Opposite page: Police arrest picketers at the White House Woman's Suffrage Demonstration, 1917.

The bitter issue of race marred even close friendships within the suffrage movement.

Ida B. Wells was a prominent journalist who had gained respect through her bold anti-lynching campaigns. She had organized the Alpha Suffrage Club, the first of many for black women in the country.

Wells clashed with her friend Susan B. Anthony over the role of blacks in the suffrage movement.

"Miss Anthony was a great friend. Once when I was at her home working on some article, she told her secretary to help me with my correspondence. When Susan found the secretary had not done so, she asked why not, and the secretary said she would not take orders from a colored woman. Susan immediately fired the secretary.... But despite Susan's beliefs, she defended the suffrage movement for ignoring racial injustice. For her, all wrongs would be righted when women voted. She had endeavored to make me see that for the sake of 'expediency,' one had often to stoop to conquer on this color question."
—Ida B. Wells

Racism within the suffrage movement reached a critical moment in 1913. Suffragists had planned a strategic march on Washington to put their issue before the eyes of the country. Ida B. Wells demanded to be included as an equal.

"The march took place the day before Wilson's inauguration—organized by Alice Paul. I was told I could not march with the all-white Chicago suffragists for fear of offending the South. That word 'expediency' was heard again. I was told I could bring up the rear; I would have none of it. When the march started, I appeared out of the crowd of onlookers as the Chicago delegation made its way past me. I simply joined in and marched as I pleased."
—Ida B. Wells

"When black women get the vote, it will find her a tower of strength of which poets have never sung, orators have never spoken, and scholars have never written."
—Nannie Helen Burroughs,
teacher and founder of the Nannie Burroughs School

"We thought that the vote was the key to being able to get education, which is, again, the key to getting out of domestic work. We thought that the vote was the key to getting the proper jobs. The National Association of Colored Women, which was founded in 1896, had a suffrage department. As a number of black women have said, if white women needed the vote, boy, did we need it."
—Paula Giddings

Above: *Ida B. Wells* **Opposite page, top:** *Suffragists wage a banner campaign at the White House gates, using President Wilson's war message as ammunition, circa 1914.*

Despite the exclusion of black women, the 1913 march on Washington made its point for democracy.

By 1916, all of the Western states had granted women the right to vote. But only a constitutional amendment would guarantee the vote to women throughout the country. For that, Congress had to act.

But President Wilson had another battle on his hands—World War I.

The irony that President Wilson was calling for democracy in Europe but not at home had not escaped the Suffragists.

"If we can send our sons in battle for the right of foreigners to self-rule, then we women should have that same right at home. Are not American women as good as French men?"

The war made women even more determined to gain their rights. While Carrie Chapman Catt continued to work on a state-by-state basis, Alice Paul led a federal campaign of relentless daily picketing in front of the White House. President Wilson soon tired of the harassment. It was October 20, 1917.

Dozens of suffragists were arrested and sentenced to prison in the Occoquan Workhouse, a notorious woman's jail just outside of Washington, D.C. Alice Paul was separated from the others and put in the district jail. All the women demanded to be treated as political prisoners. When that was denied, they embarked on a hunger strike. Infuriated, the prison officials retaliated with the torture of force-feeding.

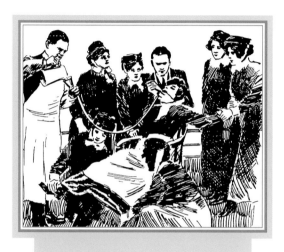

"Yesterday was a bad day for me in feeding. I am vomiting continuously during the process. The tube has developed an irritation somewhere that is painful. Don't let them tell you that we take this well. Miss Paul vomits much. We think of the coming feeding all day. It is horrible."
—Rose Winslow,
suffragist

"From the moment we undertook the hunger strike, a policy of unremitting intimidation began. I was taken to a psychopathic ward and the door was removed from my cell. The matron was told to keep an eye on me all night, and every few minutes she would shine a flashlight in my eyes, making sleep impossible.

"All night and during the day there would be cries and shrieks and moans from the patients. It was terrifying. I said to myself—I have to endure this. I have got to live through this.

"I was interviewed by the prison psychiatrists and I realized I was only one signature away from being committed to an insane asylum. They kept asking me about President Wilson. They wanted to know if I regarded him as a personal enemy. Paranoia or a perse-cution complex would be enough to commit me to St. Elizabeth's.

"I said there was nothing personal in the President's opposition to suffrage. I believe I have never in my life before feared anything or any human being, but I confess I was afraid of Dr. Gannon, the jail physician. I dreaded the hour of his visit."

—Alice Paul

Paul's tactics proved sound. After thirty-seven days, the prisoners were released without explanation. The powerful persis-tence of suffragists, along with World War I in Europe, turned the tide in favor of American women.

President Wilson did an about-face and urged Congress to pass the Nineteenth Amendment. He needed a unified America and the unconditional support of women to continue the war.

*Top: Occoquan "Psychopathic Ward" where Alice Paul was confined, 1917 **Right:** Alice Paul **Opposite page, right:** Vida Milholland, suffragist, arrested on the Fourth of July.*

Both houses of Congress passed the amendment. Now it was up to the states to ratify. Thirty-six *yes* votes were needed. Many suffragists still feared the amendment would go down in defeat. As tension mounted, Alice Paul optimistically sewed a star on her suffrage banner for each of the ratifying states.

On August 18, 1920, just one more state was needed. It was up to Tennessee. A *no* would deal a fatal setback. A *yes* would make the Nineteenth Amendment the law of the land.

Tennessee Senator Harry Burn received a letter from his mother.

"Hurrah! and vote for suffrage and don't keep them in doubt. I've been watching to see how you stood, but have noticed nothing yet. Don't forget to be a good boy and help Mrs. Catt put the Rat in ratification."

Harry Burn listened to his mother.

Above: *Alice Paul gives a speech to the National Woman's Party.*

*"It took George Washington six years to rectify man's griev-
ances by war. But it took seventy-two years to establish women's
rights by law. At least one thousand legal enactments were necessary, and every one was a struggle against ignorant opposition.
Woman suffrage is a long story of hard work and heartache,
crowned by victory."*

—*Carrie Chapman Catt, 1920*

When the vote was won, it was won for all women, regardless of race.

With the ballot in hand, the question for many women was:

What's next?

CHAPTER ELEVEN

Eleanor Roosevelt

"The women know that life must go on and that the needs of life must be met, and it is their courage and determination which, time and again, have pulled us through worse crises than the present one."

—Eleanor Roosevelt

*I*t was 1929. The stock market crashed, plunging the United States into the Great Depression. The people of this country cast their votes for change when they elected Franklin Delano Roosevelt president in 1932. What they didn't bargain for was his wife, Eleanor.

"She was, I think, the heart of the FDR years. She received I don't know how many letters every day, and she would refer them to one department or another. It got to be so that the cabinet members got just a little bit weary of my Aunt Eleanor, and they would say, 'uh oh, here's another letter from Eleanor again—somebody we should help, somebody that's in trouble.'"

—Eleanor Roosevelt,
First Lady Eleanor Roosevelt's niece

"Dear Mrs. Roosevelt, I know you are overwhelmed with requests for help, and if my plea cannot be recognized I'll understand it because you have so many others, all worthy. But I'm not asking for myself alone. It is as a potential mother, as one woman to another..."

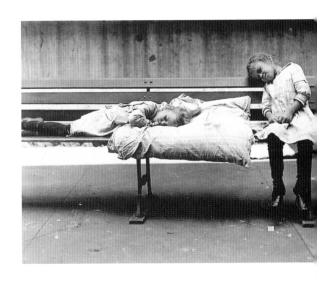

"If the women are willing to do things because it's going to help their neighbors, I think we'll win out. We'll win out not because of government, not even because of our leaders, but because as a people, we've had a vision, and we've worked for it, and we've seen it through."

—Eleanor Roosevelt

"She really is the heart of that movement to reform a devastated economic system. She is the heart of that movement which says there could be a situation that would guarantee housing for everybody, health care for everybody, education for everybody, dignity and decency for everybody."

—Blanche Cook,
historian

"The experience which is the most valuable is the experience of doing things for yourselves—getting self-confidence, getting the feeling that you stand on your own two feet."

—Eleanor Roosevelt,
in a speech to the Girl Scouts, 9 April 1957

Eleanor Roosevelt's self-confidence was hard won. Her childhood was shaped by her absent, alcoholic father and her distant, judgmental mother.

"She always thought of herself as homely because her mother thought of her as homely and said to her when she was six perhaps, 'You have no looks, so see to it that you achieve manners.'"
—Blanche Cook

Eleanor astonished her family by making what was called a great marriage. Franklin Delano Roosevelt was her fifth cousin once removed, and he was considered a "catch."

"It's a very impassioned and ardent love story. They have a secret engagement for three years because Sarah Delano Roosevelt really didn't want her son to marry anybody; she really made it very tough for them to get married. But they did get married. And then very quickly, within six years, they had about five children. Eleanor Roosevelt wrote at one point that for ten years she was either getting pregnant or having a child, or being forever with child."
—Blanche Cook

But it was a personal betrayal that changed Eleanor Roosevelt's life.

As she was busy raising her family, FDR was in Washington as Secretary of the Navy during World War I. In 1918, he returned home from a trip overseas. As Eleanor unpacked his luggage, she found a packet of letters.

"To her great dismay she discovered that FDR was having an affair with Lucy Mercer, who was her friend and social secretary. And when she discovered that, she was really devastated and offered FDR a divorce."
—Blanche Cook

A divorce would have cost FDR his political career. Family and advisors kept them together.

"The Lucy Mercer affair is a tremendous turning point in Eleanor Roosevelt's life. In odd ways, her knowledge of the affair frees her to pursue her own life, and she makes the connection that you cannot live through other people."
—Blanche Cook

"During the war, I became a more tolerant person. Far less sure of my own beliefs and methods of action, but I think more determined to try for certain ultimate objectives. I knew more about the human heart, which had been somewhat veiled in mystery."
—Eleanor Roosevelt

Franklin Delano Roosevelt's career took off, and Eleanor Roosevelt looked beyond her family for fulfillment. She joined the League of Women Voters and became very active in Democratic party politics. She worked to end child labor, advocated protectionism for working women, and, in the aftermath of World War I, became an ardent supporter of world peace. When her husband was elected president, Eleanor Roosevelt got the opportunity to forge her own political agenda.

FDR named Frances Perkins Secretary of Labor, the first time in American history that a woman had the chance to serve on a president's cabinet. Perkins was one of a dozen women in the new administration, a group that became known as "The Network." The First Lady was at the center of a growing New Deal sisterhood.

"Eleanor Roosevelt was a gift to all the women in Washington, the women who flocked to the New Deal agencies along with the men. She was very generous with giving her name—and also access to the White House—to women, many of whom she had been working with in New York since the 1920s."

—Susan Ware,
historian

"When I wanted help on some point, Mrs. Roosevelt gave me the opportunity to sit by the President at dinner, and the matter was settled before we finished our soup."

—Molly Dewson,
Democratic Party Committee

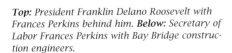

Top: President Franklin Delano Roosevelt with Frances Perkins behind him. **Below:** Secretary of Labor Frances Perkins with Bay Bridge construction engineers.

Eleanor Roosevelt was, in many ways, a very different sort of First Lady than any of her predecessors. She spoke directly to the American people—particularly women—through a daily newspaper column called "My Day."

"One of the things that disturbed her was the way that working women were often blamed for the Depression. With so many unemployed, sometimes people would say, 'Well, there are thirteen million women working and there are thirteen million people unemployed. Presto. All we need to do is fire the women and we've solved the problem.' And she would say, 'But it's not so simple. The kinds of jobs of the men who are unemployed are coal miners and heavy construction. The kinds of jobs that women have are nursemaids and social workers and playground supervisors. You can't just have the men transfer into the female jobs.' So that when someone said, 'Give up your job,' they could say, 'But Eleanor Roosevelt says that women have a right to work.'"

—Susan Ware

Eleanor Roosevelt paid for her activism. She was often cruelly criticized in the media with a nastiness previously reserved for men.

"People are always attacking her as being the one who wore the pants. 'Isn't it time to get the pants off of Eleanor and onto Franklin?' was a routine statement even within the administration."

—Blanche Cook

Mrs. Roosevelt was also criticized for earning her own living while in the White House. She insisted on being paid for her writing, saying that too often women's work was devalued.

"Eleanor Roosevelt was most controversial for her stands on civil rights, and here she was light years ahead of her husband, of Washington D.C. in the 1930s, and really the country as a whole. Civil rights was not on the national agenda."
—Susan Ware

"Blacks were not treated as equal citizens in this country, and she was very aware of that and wanted to change it. And she simply decided in her mind that she would live her own life the way she believed it should be led."
—Eleanor Roosevelt,
Eleanor Roosevelt's niece

"Eleanor Roosevelt, unlike most white Americans in the 1930s, pushed herself to confront the racism that she had grown up with. Most of the women she worked with were white. And so it was a challenge to her when she began working with black women like Mary McLeod Bethune in the 1930s."
—Susan Ware

Mary McLeod Bethune became head of the Negro Division of the National Youth Administration in 1935. Before coming to Washington, Bethune had earned a reputation as an avid supporter of universal education and had founded dozens of schools throughout the South, as well as a college that still bears her name. She had also co-founded the National Council of Negro Women.

"I felt that if these talented white women were working at such responsible jobs at a time of national crisis, I could do the same thing. I visualized dozens of Negro women coming after me, filling positions of high trust and strategic importance."
—Mary McLeod Bethune

Top: *Mary McLeod Bethune*
Right: *Bethune with a group of students.*

"Mary McLeod Bethune was one of the main organizers of the blacks in what was called the 'kitchen cabinet of the Roosevelt Administration.' There were a number of black subcabinet members there, and she organized them into a force. So she became a very influential and very important person."

—Paula Giddings,
historian

"Eleanor Roosevelt learned to greet Mary McLeod Bethune in the same way she would greet her white friends, often with a little peck on the cheek. This was quite a strong statement coming from the First Lady, that she would greet a woman of color the same way she would greet a white woman. It was also very disturbing to southern Democrats, who were a large part of her husband's political constituency."

—Susan Ware

"Eleanor Roosevelt was consistent in her opposition to segregation and to racial injustice."

—Blanche Cook

"One of the interesting things to me about Eleanor Roosevelt is that she's at least trying to struggle with these issues of race. She was not born to be a liberal, but seemed to at least work at it."

—Paula Giddings

When the acclaimed contralto Marian Anderson was refused use of the American Legion Theater in Washington D.C., an outraged Eleanor Roosevelt resigned from the Daughters of the American Revolution and was instrumental in moving the concert to the Lincoln Memorial.

Eleanor Roosevelt was First Lady for almost thirteen years, until her husband's sudden death in 1945. After the White House, she continued her public advocacy throught her involvement in Democratic party policy and by laying the groundwork for other women politicians. She also represented the United States at the U.N., culminating in her support of the United Nations Universal Declaration of Human Rights. These principles would be tested to their fullest with the civil rights struggle, which was just heating up when Eleanor Roosevelt died in 1962.

CHAPTER TWELVE

"Oh, Freedom"

"If I look back and think about the women in the early sixties in the Movement the Civil Rights Movement, we were sisters to one another and family and mothers. I guess women feel that we've been caretakers of our families and children and so on. But we have a deep feeling about how the social ills are wrong in a community or a country, and how it affects us. I think we are sensitive to that."

—Unita Blackwell,
civil rights activist

"We are confronted primarily with a moral issue. It is as old as the scriptures, and is as clear as the American Constitution. The heart of the question is whether all Americans are to be afforded equal rights and equal opportunities."
—John F. Kennedy

"The injustice of saying to a person, 'You cannot be a registered voter'—I mean that's basic; you know, that's basic."
—Victoria Gray

"In the sixties, you could not drive on the same road with white people. You had to pull off onto the side if you saw them coming. You couldn't pass a white person."
—Unita Blackwell

"When you're thirsty and say you want some water, you've got to make sure you're drinking out of the fountain that says 'black,' as opposed to the other fountain."
—Victoria Gray,
civil rights activist

"Segregation was humiliating. To have to use the back door, or not to be able to sit at a lunch counter at Woolworth's or Walgreen's..."
—Diane Nash,
civil rights activist

By the early 1960s, black Americans had said enough is enough. In cities all across the South, their frustrations were met with violence. The Civil Rights Movement made fighters and leaders out of ordinary people. But the women have often been overlooked.

"The reason, I guess, that we never saw the women in the Civil Rights Movement on the forefront is because we always pushed our men out front. We, as black women, didn't get our due either, but we were there, as leaders."

—Unita Blackwell

"People don't realize that it was the women in the Civil Rights Movement who kept it going. They were the ones who went marching. They were the ones who cooked the meals. They were the ones who gave out the leaflets. They were the ones who were at the mass meetings. They were the ones who decided to take in some totally poverty-stricken civil rights workers. The work of the women has really been unsung, and without them, I'm not sure there would've been a movement this size."

—Dorothy Zellner, civil rights activist

One of the unsung women leaders of the sixties was Ella
Baker, who became an inspiration for a generation just finding
its voice. Baker founded the Student Non-Violent Coordinating
Committee, or SNCC, in 1960 to organize the efforts of students
who were staging sit-ins independently, all over the South. SNCC
brought together idealistic young men and women from all over
the country.

*"I met Ella Baker in the spring of 1960. She was Executive
Director of the Southern Christian Leadership Conference at the time.
She and the SCLC sponsored a conference of the students of various
campuses at which the Student Non-Violent Coordinating Committee
was founded.*

*"She was serious about democracy. She really believed in people
controlling their own destiny and doing things as a group and everyone having a voice."*

—Diane Nash

*"She is the reason why the student movement exists. She
believed in young people.*

*"The people in SNCC were really young. I was twenty-two or
twenty-three when I went south, and I was one of the older people.
And she said, 'No, let them create their own organization. Let them
do what they feel is necessary.'*

*"She was a democrat, small d. She actually believed people had
incredible power over their lives. And she often said, 'strong people
don't need strong leaders.'"*

—Dorothy Zellner

SNCC's loose democratic structure gave women a unique opportunity to rise as leaders. Diane Nash was just twenty-two years old when she risked her life leading lunch counter sit-ins.

"One particular day we had sit-ins at about half a dozen restaurants and lunch counters. My picture had been in the local newspaper, and I heard one young, white teenager say, 'That's Diane Nash, I saw her picture in the paper. She's the one to get.' And I got so frightened—I was really paralyzed with fear, until I realized that the fear was preventing me from focusing on my job, and on what I was doing. And I was able to find a way to get rid of the fear."

—*Diane Nash*

Nash was eventually arrested for attempting to integrate a Mississippi lunch counter.

Diane Nash was sentenced for contempt of court and spent ten days in jail.

"I was expecting a baby—I was five months pregnant. People said, 'How can you think about surrendering to go to jail? Because it'll mean that you'll have your child in jail.' And I said, 'Well, now I have a stake in the future, I have children who will have to live in this society. This will be a black child born in Mississippi, so if the child is born in the jail building or not, it will still be born in jail.'"

—*Diane Nash*

Committed young people like Diane Nash traveled throughout the South, organizing, educating, and registering people to vote. Rural Mississippi was the Movement's biggest challenge. But there they found women of exceptional courage, including Fannie Lou Hamer.

"Mrs. Hamer, to me, personified what people are really capable of. There are people that society considers totally ordinary—Mrs. Hamer was a sharecropper her whole life until her forties, but look at what she was capable of. She was capable of this incredible courage."

—Dorothy Zellner

"I think the thing that really stood out for me about Fannie Lou was the stand that she took when she went in to get registered. When she got back to the plantation that night, not really realizing, I guess, the seriousness of this whole thing, she was faced with the plantation owner, who met her immediately and demanded that she do one of two things."

—Victoria Gray

"Mr. Marlowe told me that I would have to go down and withdraw my registration or leave, because they wasn't ready for that in Mississippi. And I said, 'Mr. Marlowe, I'm trying to register for myself,' so I had to leave that same night."

—Fannie Lou Hamer

Sixty miles away, in another small town in Mississippi, SNCC workers found Unita Blackwell. When she went to register, her troubles came at the courthouse, not the plantation.

Black Mississippians had virtually no political representation. The delegation to the 1964 Democratic National Convention was to be all white. In response, the integrated Mississippi Freedom Democratic Party was formed. Victoria Gray made the announcement:

"We have organized into the Mississippi Freedom Democratic Party. We are holding a Freedom registration drive throughout the state, encouraging every Negro and white who wants a stake in his political future to prove it by getting his name on a Freedom registration book. We have scheduled precinct meetings and district caucuses. And, on August 6th, here in Jackson, we will hold our state convention. At that time, we will elect a slate of delegates to the national convention in Atlantic City. And when that convention meets, we will present ourselves for seating as the only democratically constituted body of Mississippi citizens worthy of taking part in that convention's business."

"I saw the hate in the eyes of the whites. We'd been seeing it all our lives, but, you know, they were so angry about us just going over trying to register to vote. And I knew that this must have been important. I vowed that day that nothing from nothing leaves nothing. We didn't have nothing, but if I had to die, I was going to be dying trying to register to vote."
—Unita Blackwell

"I do intend to vote..., because it's very important to have the people represented. And I want somebody to represent me."
—Unita Blackwell, 1965, being questioned at a news conference

At the Atlantic City convention, the Freedom Democratic Party was refused seating. Television reporters questioned Fannie Lou Hamer, one of the Mississippi delegates:

And would you identify yourself for us please?
My name is Mrs. Fannie Lou Hamer. I'm the Vice Chairman of the Freedom Democratic Party.

Where did you get the credentials to get into the building tonight, Mrs. Hamer?
Some loyal friends of ours gave us an invitation to come in. We sat with them awhile, but we wanted to sit in our own state.

Do you have any kind of credentials that will get you into these seats?
No, we don't—only as American citizens.

They pleaded their case before the convention's Credentials Committee. Fannie Lou Hamer was their spokesperson:
"If the Freedom Democratic Party is not seated now, I question America. Is this America? The land of the free, and the home of the brave? Where we have to sleep with our telephones off of the hook because our lives be threatened daily, because we want to live as decent human beings in America."

President Johnson was infuriated by Mrs. Hamer's impassioned plea for justice. He demanded that the three networks switch immediately to the White House, in effect silencing Mrs. Hamer.

The Mississippi Freedom Democratic Party was offered two seats at the convention. They refused to compromise and were not seated, but the effort was not a loss; they had captured the nation's attention. Fannie Lou Hamer went on to become a delegate to the 1968 convention and remained politically active until her death in 1977.

Mississippi Freedom Summer changed history and the lives of the women who came of political age that year.

"My older son said to me one day, 'Mom, we really would like to have you stay home with us.' I said, 'Yes, I know that.' And I feel like what I was really trying to convey to him was that as important as it was for me to be there with them, it was far more important for them to live their lives in a different way than we had to live our lives. And that's what I tried to say to him: 'Mommie's doing this so that you will not have to do what I'm doing, that life will be different for you.'" —Victoria Gray

Victoria Gray is now Professor of Theology at the University of Virginia.

"The Movement had a way of reaching inside you and bringing out things that even you didn't know were there, like courage." —Diane Nash

Diane Nash, grandmother of two, lectures at colleges and universities.

"As a white woman and a northerner, I feel extremely fortunate to have been involved in the Civil Rights Movement. And I was lucky enough to know that this was a moment when history was being made, and I wanted to be part of it." —Dorothy Zellner

Dorothy Zellner works as a legal aid for civil rights in New York City.

"We didn't know what it was like to lay down and go to sleep and have the quietness just to rest. And now, some people want to know what's different. We do have problems. The difference is that it's quieter. And I go to sleep and I'm not worried that I might not wake up." —Unita Blackwell

In 1976, Unita Blackwell became the first black woman mayor in Mississippi. She retired in 1993.

LADY MAYOR OF MAYERSVILLE

Rights worker becomes Mississippi's first black woman mayor

"Looking back on the Movement, there were times, many of them, that were really difficult—the times that you really knew there was a good possibility of being killed or beaten or seriously hurt. However, I feel blessed to have been at the right place at the right time and to have become involved with the Movement, because I've led a different kind of life because of it.

"I think the Movement gave me a sense of what a human being is supposed to be about—being involved with my fellow human beings on this planet and making this society a better place to be. That was important to me."

—Diane Nash

CHAPTER THIRTEEN

Changing The Laws

"The chief characteristic of women's history is that it is lost and rediscovered, lost again and re-rediscovered. It forces each generation to reinvent all of history by itself."

—*Gloria Steinem,*
author

On August 26, 1970, fifty years to the day after women got the vote, their daughters and granddaughters marched in the streets of New York, continuing the fight for equality.

"A lot of the things you see now, you never would have seen before—women marching in the streets for themselves. We've marched for every other movement that exists."
—Gloria Steinem, 1970

Women wanted change—change in the laws that paid them less money than men for equal work, change in the laws that said a woman's body was not her own, change in the rules that kept women silent about their most personal experiences.

By the 1970s, it was clear America was going through the throes of a social revolution. Women were speaking out as never before in a strong, collective voice. The media called it the "Women's Movement," but women called it *life.*

"Once we had this revolutionary inkling that women were human beings, we had a lot of issues. We began to name the issues, such as sexual harassment. It was just called life. It didn't even have a name until the mid-seventies; women named it. Displaced homemakers was just called life. Battered women was just called life. All those terms were invented by the Women's Movement."

—Gloria Steinem

Women did speak-outs, populist education, and protests. Secrets were swept from the back of closets and held up to the light of public debate.

"I went as a reporter to cover an abortion hearing. And I will never forget that night as long as I live, because I heard women stand up and tell the truth in public for the first time in my life. What it was like to have to go out and enter an illegal underground or try to find an illegal abortion. For me, that was the moment when the light bulb began to come on. Because I, too, had had an abortion when I was about twenty-two, and told no one. Absolutely not one single human being, except the physician."

—Gloria Steinem

It seemed as if overnight the long silence about abortion was finally over.

In 1973, a case out of Texas that sought to make abortion legal—*Roe* versus *Wade*—was argued in front of the Supreme Court.

"I was just a few years out of law school, in my twenties still, when I went to the U.S. Supreme Court. When I started the case, I never thought it was a U.S. Supreme Court case. In fact, I think if anyone had been circling the globe in the late sixties and looked down and said, 'Which person down there would possibly do this case?' no one would have picked me.

"I was the daughter of a Methodist minister, had been very active in very traditional things. I was the president of the Future Homemakers of America. I had never done anything that would make someone think I would be the one. But I knew that on that case would rest the future for many women, and that what the court did would be so critical in how history would play out. So I wanted more than I had ever wanted anything to win that case."

—Sarah Weddington,
attorney

The decision was handed down on January 22, 1973.

"The phone rang. It was a member of the press, who called to say that we had won Roe *versus* Wade *on a vote of seven to two."*

—Sarah Weddington

One woman's legal fight had changed history for all women. *Roe* versus *Wade* continues to generate heated debate. In 1989, the decision was nearly overturned by the Supreme Court, and a woman's right to privacy and control over her own body remains a divisive issue for many women and men. But the long silence was over. Speaking out proved to be the first step toward change.

"Before Roe *versus* Wade, *women were reduced to the indignities of back alleys and illegal places. They had to escape the laws of the states where they lived; they were declared criminals. Once* Roe versus Wade *was decided, they were freed from the indignities of illegal abortion and for the first time had the dignity of being recognized as the appropriate persons to make their own decisions, and to carry them out."*

—Sarah Weddington

In the early seventies, Susan Brownmiller helped organize speak-outs and conferences on the issue of rape. The goal—to end decades of guilt and shame.

"In the course of organizing a conference, I realized that what I wanted to do—my special contribution to the Women's Movement—would be to go to the libraries and reconstruct rape's history from biblical times to the present, because nobody had ever thought that rape had a history. And my feeling was that once rape had a history, and it was down there on paper, we could begin to deny it its future."

—Susan Brownmiller,
historian

"Within a couple of years we began to see tremendous changes in the state legislatures. They were revising their rape statutes to take our thinking into account. They dropped the corroboration requirement, which said that a victim had to have an eyewitness to the rape. They put into effect the rape shield laws to limit the cross-examination of the victim on the stand. I mean, the lawyer would grill the victim as to her prior sexual history and make it look like she clearly solicited the sexual act and it was consensual."
—Susan Brownmiller

Significant changes were made. Rape crisis centers were started. Law enforcement officials now sent policewomen to talk to rape victims, and a woman's past sexual history was no longer admissible in court.

Subjects that were once kept within the family were now talked about openly—on television, among friends, in magazines, and in courts of law.

A woman named Martha Warren had been married twenty-two months when a night of violence sent her to the police.

"I said no, and I meant no. I did not want to do anything. I wanted to be left alone. He choked me, beat my head against the wall; there was blood all over the walls, the bed."
—Martha Warren Golloway

She had no idea that she would change the way the law looked at marriage.

"When I went to talk to the judge, I started telling him what happened to me. He asked me was I raped, and I said, well, I didn't know that I could call it that because I'm married to him. And he told me there wasn't any law that he knew of that wouldn't call it rape if that's what happened, and he asked me would I swear to it—that I was raped. And I said, yes, I would swear to it. It was as if a total stranger had done it to me. In my eyes, it wasn't my husband."
—Martha Warren Golloway

Legal precedent had held that rape within marriage was impossible because marriage implied consent. Legally, marriage was the union of two people into one—the husband—and the courts had historically maintained that no man could rape himself.

The Georgia Supreme Court sentenced Martha Warren's husband to fifteen years in prison. Today, spousal rape is a crime in all fifty states.

"I know that because of what I did in the past, I did change the laws and I can do something about it. I had the strength; I don't know how I found it, but I found the strength to stand up for myself."
—Martha Warren Golloway

The final decades of this century are filled with similar stories—women speaking out, standing up, and fighting back.

In 1990, the issue of sexual harassment suddenly entered front-page headlines. A Supreme Court nominee, Clarence Thomas, was accused of sexual harassment by a former co-worker, Anita Hill.

"It is only after a great deal of agonizing consideration and sleepless nights that I am able to talk of these unpleasant matters to anyone but my closest friends. "I thought that by saying 'no' and explaining my reasons, my employer would abandon his social suggestions. However, to my regret, in the following weeks he continued to ask me out."

—Anita Hill,
at the Clarence Thomas
confirmation hearings

This very public debate polarized Americans and resulted in nothing less than a full-scale reevaluation of the issues of harassment, as well as the political representation of women.

"The Anita Hill hearing may be the first time in the history of the country that popular culture focused on women's experience in prime time for three days."

—Gloria Steinem

"I think that the Anita Hill hearings, and the way she was treated, and the way the Senate looked, and the emotions that were touched by it inside women, just changed them. And it made them realize that you really can't have a representative democracy if you don't have women at the highest levels of government.

—Senator Barbara Boxer,
(D) California

In 1992, the Supreme Court—now for the first time with two women, Sandra Day O'Connor and Ruth Bader Ginsburg, serving on the bench—expanded the definition of sexual harassment to include language and a hostile environment. That decision was both a moral and a practical victory for women.

As the twentieth century draws to a close, certain advances are clear. No matter what side women and men take on any specific issue, all Americans can take heart that the long silence is over.

"The women who started the suffragist and abolitionist wave didn't live long enough to see women even get the vote. And I won't live long enough to see a society in which sex and race aren't allowed to determine all human futures. But if the flap of a butterfly wing—as even the most hard-nosed physicist now admits—can change the weather hundreds of miles away, then everything we do matters. And it matters not only now, but it matters in the long term."

—Gloria Steinem

VALLEY EDITION

Los Angeles Times

TUESDAY, JUNE 15, 1993
COPYRIGHT 1993/THE TIMES MIRROR COMPANY / F / CCI / 152 PAGES

DAILY 25¢
DESIGNATED AREAS HIGHER

RCULATION:
8,353 DAILY / 1,521,197 SUNDAY

VALLEY NEWSWATCH

T MAKING IT: The Writers ld says movie and TV studios ed more minority and women ters between 1987 and 1991. "substantial barriers to equal portunity persist" **(F1).** The ks of women and minorities reased at Disney, Warner s. and NBC in Burbank and versal in Universal City, but men still receive lower pay at ny studios. . . . The widest der gap, with women making cents for each dollar earned by le writers, was at MTM in dio City.

OD THAT DELIVERS: OK, s may sound strange, but is it sible that the romaine and tercress salad at Caioti, a ky restaurant in Laurel Canh, sends overdue pregnant men into welcome labor? At st two Valley women say it ppened to them **(E1).** . . . en medical types concede it's . impossible. Said one: "I've rned not to pooh-pooh things mingly off the wall."

FDA: Vitamin Claims Need to Be Proven

By MARLENE CIMONS
TIMES STAFF WRITER

WASHINGTON—In a controversial decision, the Food and Drug Administration announced Monday that manufacturers must have scientific proof of the benefits of dietary supplements—vitamins, minerals. amino acids and other nutritional substances—before they can make health claims on product labels.

The decision holds the dietary supplement industry to the same standards that the agency set for health claims about food.

The new rules, which are now subject to 60 days of public comment, mean that scientific experts must agree about the value of a **Please see VITAMINS, A22**

U.N. Expands Battle Against Somali Warlord

By ART PINE and TODD SHIELDS

Clinton Picks Moderate Judge Ruth Ginsburg for High Court

■ **Judiciary:** President calls the former women's rights activist a healer and consensus builder. Her nomination is expected to win easy Senate approval.

By PAUL RICHTER
TIMES STAFF WRITER

WASHINGTON—In a surpr ending to a tortuous three-mo search, President Clinton on Mc day nominated Ruth Bader Gi burg, an appeals court judge a former women's rights activist, a Supreme Court justice, mak her the first appointment to high court by a Democratic adm istration in 26 years.

Ginsburg, 60, who serves on U.S. Court of Appeals for District of Columbia, was haile Clinton in a Rose Garden cere ny. He said that she is a mode who has "proven herself to healer" and consensus builder who has put her convictions deeds during a long career as professor, advocate and judge.

Clinton, who appeared mo tarily moved to tears by Ginst brief acceptance remarks, said in her efforts on behalf of wo rights, Ginsburg "has compil

Image & *Popular Culture*

*A*mericans have always placed tremendous emphasis on women's appearance, sometimes at the expense of their skills, intelligence, and achievements. However, as the twentieth century has worn on, the definitions of beauty for women have broadened and diversified. With greater opportunities for women in sports, and with the increased respect and attention paid to women in the arts, women have adopted a wider range of role models.

"Image and Popular Culture" examines the way representations of women in the media, popular culture, and the arts have changed over the course of the years. The voices and stories of great women such as Claire McCardell, Chris Evert, Zora Neale Hurston, Maya Angelou, Amelia Earhart, Lucille Ball, Bessie Smith, and Georgia O'Keefe describe the steps women have taken to change their image and the way they see themselves.

CHAPTER FOURTEEN

A Change of Clothes

"The history of mankind is, in large measure, the history of woman's beauty."

—Photoplay, *March 1922*

"She must be essentially woman. Feminine curves, suggested by chiffons and laces, are more alluring than angular bones."

—Time, *September 1944*

The confining fashions of the early twentieth century were designed to exaggerate the female figure. Tightly cinched, with long, billowy skirts, the clothes were hardly the sort to encourage any independent actions.

Most American women were still wearing corsets—torso prisons that were an unpleasant surprise for arriving immigrant women who were forced to lace up soon after landing.

Some thought a popular corset model died from wearing one. Whether or not her corset was the culprit, the public believed her tightly cinched torso took her breath away—literally.

When the United States entered World War I in 1916, the war office said that if American women were released from their corsets, twenty-eight thousand tons of steel would be freed—enough to build and furnish two battleships. American women were eager to perform their patriotic duties.

Dr. Mary Walker was a New York surgeon at the turn of the twentieth century who thought that women badly needed a change of clothes.

"It should be the object of dress to save vitality, instead of expending it in the foolish and wicked manner that fashion dictates. Dress reform for women is of paramount importance. The want of the ballot is but a toy in comparison!

"The snug fit of the dress or corset prevents freedom of motion, of respiration, digestion, assimilative circulation of the blood and the nervo-vital fluid. It prevents the freedom of the muscles of the lower part of the chest and the upper part of the legs, producing a weariness of the bony structure."

—Dr. Mary Walker

Walker dared to wear what felt good, even at the risk of ridicule.

"The pants are made like men's and are either buttoned to the waist of an undersuit or arranged with the usual suspenders. The dress is made to hang free of the body, the waist and skirt of one piece like a sack cloth and falling to the knees, thus preventing it being stomped upon while descending stairs. The time is coming when every woman will dress in this style for the advantages are too evident to be much longer overlooked."

—Dr. Mary Walker

Top: *Doctor Mary Walker attired comfortably.*
Opposite page, top: *Corset tightening ritual.*
Opposite page, left: *Newly arrived Japanese immigrant women.* **Opposite page, middle:** *Japanese woman, cinched by a Western-style corset.*

No one was more eager to shed the corset than New York debutante Caresse Crosby, who refused to be constrained in her undergarment, or in her life.

"When I made my debut, girlish figures were being encased in a sort of box-like armor of whale bone and pink cordage. These garments were forever having to be tucked or pinned or pushed out of sight once one was dressed for a party and they were hellishly binding as well. If petting had been practiced in those days, it never could have gone very far."

—Caresse Crosby

Caresse Crosby was born in New York in 1892, into a world of privilege and tradition. But despite a rigid upbringing, Caresse was a rebel.

"'I'm not going to wear that thing tonight. It spoils the entire effect. Bring me two of my pocket handkerchiefs, some pink ribbon, the needle, thread, and some pins.' I pinned the handkerchiefs together and stitched the pink ribbons to the two points below my breast bone. The result was delicious. In the glass I saw that I was flat and I was proper. I could move and sway and dance in comfort."

—Caresse Crosby

Top: *Caresse Crosby and husband.* **Bottom:** *Diagram for the first brassiere.*

Caresse Crosby had made the first bra. She sold the patent to Warner Brothers corset company, the same Warner Brothers who later brought sound to motion pictures. Warner paid Crosby only fifteen hundred dollars for her ground-breaking invention.

"To me this seemed not only adequate but magnificent. I signed on the line and went home in opulence. I believe it couldn't have taken many years for Warner Brothers to clean up fifteen million or more."
—Caresse Crosby

Caresse Crosby's invention was the first step for women in gaining freedom from restrictive wardrobes, the same freedom that Dr. Mary Walker had demanded back when the century began.

Many women like Mary Walker believed that women's clothes should be more comfortable. All they needed now was someone to lead the way to change.

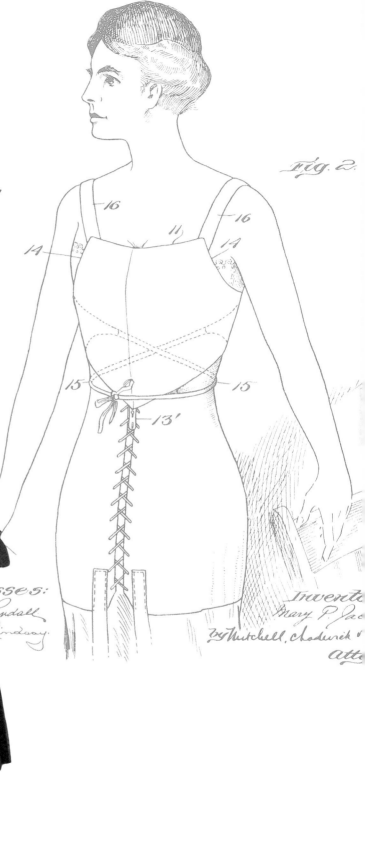

Amelia Earhart, in 1928, became the first woman to cross the Atlantic by air. In 1932, she did it again—solo—another first for a woman. Her courage, confidence, and style fascinated women and men.

"Whenever she finished a flight she always was asked various questions. And two of the most prevalent were 'Were you afraid?' And usually the answer was 'No.' And the second was, 'What did you wear?' I think she was a little surprised at the attention to her wardrobe."

—Susan Ware,
historian

"Amelia Earhart really could walk into a room today and look perfectly at home with her short tousled hair, her beautifully tailored pants, her sensible shoes, the silk scarf knotted around her neck. And I think part of her appeal was that she captured that sense of modernity."

—Susan Ware

"We were traveling light across the Atlantic in a place not built for comfort under conditions where skirts would not have been advisable and where warmth was a primary consideration. People who see pictures of the arrival of the Friendship in England will notice that I was dressed in what are popularly known as flying clothes—fleece or fur-lined overalls of either leather or heavy cloth."

—Amelia Earhart

Earhart's celebrity helped change the way American women wanted to look. All of a sudden, being comfortable and looking sporty were both attractive and feminine. Like today's celebrities, Earhart turned her fame into fortune.

"One of the things that was interesting about Amelia Earhart is that she actually had her own clothing line, which she developed in 1933 and '34. And it came out of her desire that she, and that women in general, should have comfortable clothes that they could be active women in."

—Susan Ware

DESIGNED BY
Amelia Earhart

"How I've suffered with sleeves that were too short or shoulders too tight! My clothes will be cut for comfort."

—Amelia Earhart

So was her hair. When women like Amelia Earhart cut off their long locks, the new bobbed style inspired a nationwide trend that caused many altercations. In one, a salesgirl named Helen Armstrong was fired from Marshall Field in Chicago for wearing her hair in a style that was "not dignified."

"Amelia Earhart really was a celebrity. Her accomplishments in the air were widely reported, she turned up on newsreels, she wrote magazine articles, she was widely photographed. Her image really conveyed both the excitement of aviation and the excitement of new possibilities for women."

—Susan Ware

"The department of commerce makes no difference in granting licenses to men or women. A pilot's a pilot. I hope that equality can be carried out in other fields."

—Amelia Earhart,
October 1, 1932, at the White House

Amelia Earhart carried her sense of personal freedom to the altar. In 1931, she married publisher George Palmer Putnam. Following the ceremony, Earhart kept both her name and her independence.

"One of the most unusual things about the way that Amelia Earhart approached marriage was that right before the ceremony she handed her husband-to-be a one-page statement that asked if she were not happy in a year, that he would let her go. And to his credit, he gulped, I think, and signed it."
—Susan Ware

"Dear George, please, let us not interfere with each other's work or play, for I cannot guarantee to endure the confinements of even an attractive cage."
—Amelia Earhart

On what was to be Amelia Earhart's last long-distance flight, she and a navigator set out to fly around the world at the equator. The most difficult leg was the 2,556 miles from New Guinea to a tiny speck in the mid-Pacific called Howland Island. At 8:45 AM on July 2, 1937, a garbled radio message was received. It was to be Earhart's last communication.

Her plane was believed to have crashed somewhere in the Pacific. No trace of the aircraft or its fliers has ever been found.

The debate continues as to both the meaning of her life and the circumstances of her death.

"For the women who had a chance to fly in the twenties and thirties, women like Amelia Earhart, it must have been such a sense of liberation, of freedom. She was any man's equal, she was on her own, and she must have been in heaven. It really was the closest that I can imagine to what liberation and true equality must have felt like."
—Susan Ware

"There really is not anything amazing in liking to fly. The amazing thing is that so few women, seeing what sport men are having in the air, are doing it themselves."
—Amelia Earhart

Of course, most women did not follow her into the skies, but they did follow her style.

*Top: Amelia Earhart and husband George Putnam. **Opposite page, top:** Fashion designer, Claire McCardell. **Opposite page, bottom:** Classic McCardell fashions.*

When America became involved in World War II, it meant wartime budgets, import restrictions, and shortages. American dress designer Claire McCardell capitalized on the need for moderately priced, practical clothes.

"I believe that clothes are for real women, not pedestals. They are made to be worn, to be lived in, not to walk around on showroom models who are blessed with perfect figures.

"I like to be able to zip my own zippers, hook my own eyes. I need dresses that I can wear to cook dinner in, and then come out and meet my guests. Don't you?"

—Claire McCardell

McCardell's first real commercial success came in the form of a controversial new design—"The Tent Dress." Publicity releases called it "The Monastic." The dress's stunning simplicity touched a fashion nerve, and soon half of Seventh Avenue was copying the McCardell design.

"Fashion should be fun, and whenever I am tempted to take it too seriously, I am tumbled to earth by the blunt question of a buyer: Where would you wear it?"

—Claire McCardell

"For me, the forties was about structure, and military and very hard-edged kind of suiting, and there comes Claire and her wonderful soft jersey dresses which freed the woman, liberated what the American woman's lifestyle was all about."

—Donna Karan,
fashion designer

Many of the designs we take for granted were popularized by McCardell. One of her innovations was the body suit. The body suit was originally designed in wool to provide an extra layer of warmth for girls living in college dormitories left unheated because of wartime fuel shortages.

"You know, people say to me 'You invented the body suit.' Absolutely not. All I did was take a leotard that was so common in dress and utilize it as a foundation. And that's, I think, what people wanted, the base of the foundation. She understood that, you know, she did that in her dressing as well."

—Donna Karan

Claire McCardell died of cancer at the age of fifty-two, two years after she published her book, entitled *What Shall I Wear?*

"For me, she is a place in history, a moment in time, but so modern. I think that when people think about Claire McCardell, they think she would be designing today."

—Donna Karan

"I've always designed things I needed myself. It just turns out other people need them, too."

—Claire McCardell

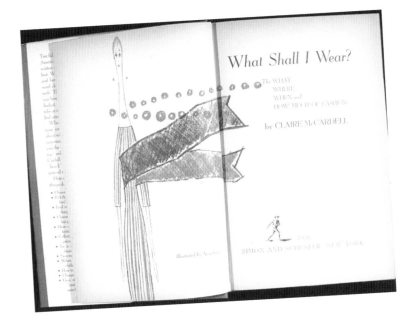

Top: *The McCardell body suit*

CHAPTER FIFTEEN

Breaking the Mold

"Hair is something that we drive ourselves crazy with as black women. And I think that goes way back to slavery days. I think the image of beauty in the United States is blonde and blue eyes. And it always has been and, I think in a lot of ways, it still is today."

—Halle Berry, actor

IHEUS. PHOTO.

The beauty business has been big business throughout the twentieth century. Makeup and hair care industries have made billions of dollars off of women's desire to look and feel good. For a few enterprising women, selling beauty has also meant financial independence.

At the turn of the twentieth century, Madam C. J. Walker believed that for black women to succeed, they needed the confidence of looking good.

Walker defied the times by excelling in business—the beauty business—one of the few fields open to women at that time. But success had been a long road. Born to former slaves on a Louisiana plantation in 1867, Madam Walker (born Sarah Breedlove) was orphaned at the age of seven, and widowed and the mother of a two-year-old daughter at age twenty-one. She kept her family together working as a laundress in St. Louis.

"As I bent over the washboard and looked at my arms buried in soapsuds, I said to myself—what are you going to do when you grow old and your back gets stiff? This set me to thinking. But with all my thinking I couldn't see how I, a poor washerwoman, was going to better my condition."

—Madam C. J. Walker

But Walker did better her condition by developing products for black women's hair, including a shampoo and conditioner which was called "Wonderful Hair Grower."

"Madam Walker was the very first one to open what we call a beauty shop, where black women could go to make themselves beautiful. I was the first one that Madam Walker ever employed and put on a payroll. I helped her open the first public shop, which was not entirely owned by her. Maybe she was in it to help a girl get started. And then the girl would either buy out the rest of the interest or pay Madam Walker back for whatever she had loaned her to get started."

—Marjorie Joyner,
associate of Madam C. J. Walker

"One night I had a dream, and in that dream a black man appeared to me and told me what to mix up for my hair. Some of the remedy was grown in Africa, but I sent for it, mixed it, put it on my scalp, and in a few weeks my hair was coming in faster than it had fallen out. I tried it on my friends; it helped them. I made up my mind I would begin to sell it."
—Madam C. J. Walker

In 1905, she moved to Denver with only $1.50 in her pocket, convinced her hair product would change her life.

"I think what happened with her is that she developed a product, she added a couple of other things, and then she put her own image on the product. And I think that's really what helped sell the product because people would look at her, they would see her as successful, they would see their own image in her, in a very African-looking woman, and then they would make the translation that they, too, could be as successful as she was. So she was, as cosmetics companies often do today, selling success in a jar."
—A'Lelia Bundles,
Madam Walker's great-great-granddaughter

"The girls and women of our race must not be afraid to take hold of business endeavors. I have made it possible for many colored women to abandon the washtub for more pleasant and profitable occupations."
—Madam C. J. Walker

In fact, Walker did more than just make it possible. She opened beauty schools that trained women to follow in her footsteps.

"She started with her first school in Pittsburgh in 1909. From there she developed at least eight or nine other schools during her lifetime around the country. She would hire a woman to be principal of the school, to train other women to learn how to do the Walker system, and from there these women could go into business for themselves."
—A'Lelia Bundles

Above: *Madam C. J. Walker*

Walker was successful, but she was not without her critics. Some felt that she was straightening black women's hair and, in doing so, promoting a white ideal of beauty.

"Even the minister in the pulpit, he'd say, you ought to stay looking like God made you instead of trying to be like white. I don't know where they got that from, but it wasn't trying to look like white, it was to give a better, well-groomed appearance."

—Marjorie Joyner

"I want the great masses of my people to take greater pride in their personal appearance and to give their hair proper attention."

—Madam C. J. Walker

> *"I had to make my own living and my own opportunity. But I made it. That is why I want to say to every Negro woman present, don't sit down and wait for the opportunities to come. You have to get up and make them."*
>
> —Madam C. J. Walker

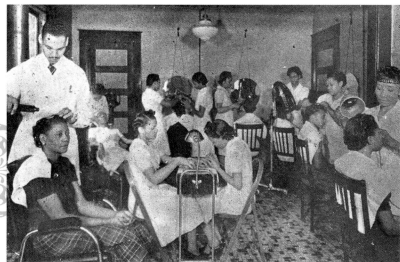

"Madam Walker knew some of the psychology of the community. In addition to straightening the hair, she was also allowing women to feel pampered. When somebody would go to a Walker beauty salon, it wasn't primarily about straightening their hair. In her eyes, it was about scalp massage and getting a massage and pampering yourself."

—A'lelia Bundles

> *"I just think it's very important that we remember that what Madam Walker represents is a woman who changed her attitude about herself, helped other women change attitudes about themselves, and therefore helped women see that they could change the world."*
>
> —A'lelia Bundles

Her knowledge of people paid off. Madam Walker sold her products internationally, traveled in a chauffeured car, built a $250,000 estate on the banks of the Hudson, and became one of the wealthiest self-made women of her time.

But the trappings of success were not Walker's priority—generosity was.

"She was a political activist. She had become involved in the anti-lynching movement. She had contributed to educational institutions around the country. She was standing up and making her views known to make life better for women and for blacks in America."

—A'lelia Bundles

The beauty business also presented opportunities for Helena Rubinstein and Elizabeth Arden, two enterprising women who created rival beauty empires.

Rubinstein, a recent immigrant from Europe, searched for a product with which to make her fortune. She ended up painting the eyes of screen vamp Theda Bara.

"Before Helena Rubinstein had her great empire, there were very few cosmetics available and very few women used them. The only women that used them were some actresses, a few people in the royal court, and some women of ill repute. My aunt brought it to every woman, every walk of life, every age."

—Mala Rubinstein,
Helena Rubinstein's niece

Florence Graham had the same idea. Aiming to sell glamour, she first changed her name to Elizabeth Arden and then painted it on a red door, the trademark of her line of make-up and her beauty salons. Her cosmetics industry was an immediate success. Even the Depression couldn't dampen her spirits. For Arden, all women needed to end hard times was the right attitude and the right make-up.

"By making the most of themselves, women could do so much to cheer the world, chase despondency, and help bring back prosperity. Come on, women of America! Let us smile. Let us work. Let us be cheerful, beautiful."

—Elizabeth Arden

The beauty industry thrived during the Depression. Money for food might have been scarce, but going without lipstick was unthinkable.

No matter what social changes swept the country, make-up never went out of style.

The business of beauty was built on encouraging women to change their looks. No one did it better or more often than Hollywood. During the heyday of the big studios, Hollywood held onto a rigid definition of beauty.

"When women of color did finally get some roles, or have a chance to strut their stuff and show what they could do, often it was within the confines of a very limiting role. Often they were trapped within the expectations that they would meet white standards, that their features, how they were presented, how they were marketed, would be very white."
—Valerie Matsumoto,
historian

"Rita Hayworth has often been idealized as a symbol of glamour for American women of the 1940s. Few realized that this red-headed, 'Anglo' sex goddess was of Spanish heritage."
—Vicki Ruiz,
historian

Margarita Cansino did not light up the box office in her early films, so her name was changed, her dark hair dyed auburn, her hairline reshaped through painful electrolysis, and her make-up altered. Rita Hayworth, sex symbol and star, was born.

Right: *Actress, Rita Hayworth*
Opposite page: *Lena Horne with Mantan Moorland.*

Ironically, although Hollywood had tried to erase Rita Hayworth's Spanish heritage, it also tried to promote another young, new talent as Spanish. Lena Horne didn't fit the mold of what producers thought a black actress should look like, so Hollywood decided to remake her into a so-called "acceptable image."

"They said, 'We've gotten so much mail from this one song you sang in Panama Hattie,' and everybody thinks, 'Oh, who's that new Spanish girl you have? Who's that girl?' And they thought they would be getting flack if people found out I was black. And I said, 'I'm sorry, I don't want to be Spanish.' None of my people are. I love Spanish people, but I unfortunately also liked my own people. So I said, 'No, I'm Lena Horne and that's it.'"
—Lena Horne,
actor

But still MGM was not satisfied that the public would accept her as she was.

"Since I didn't fit their particular mold, they did create a make-up that they thought would make me look more black than I was. And they called it Light Egyptian.

"I became so unhappy that I went to see Mrs. Hattie McDaniel, who was a great star. And I cried and I told her how outlandish I had been made to feel, and she told me, 'My darling,' she said, 'do you see the way I live?' And she had the most palatially beautiful house you'd want to see. And she said, 'I wear two hats. When I go to the studio, I wear my bandanna, and when I'm at home and go out to tea, I wear a Lily Daché bonnet.' And she said, 'If you have children and you have rent to pay, you work where you can.'"
—Lena Horne

The indignities continued. A prime role for a light-skinned black woman was Julie, the mulatto wife in *Show Boat*. But MGM refused to give the role to Lena Horne, choosing instead to put Horne's Light Egyptian make-up on Ava Gardner.

"It depleted me. It depleted my sense of worth. I was so busy having to react to their attitudes that it lessened my strength as a person."

—Lena Horne

Struggling to meet someone else's ideal of beauty can do that to a woman. Today women spend over twenty-five billion dollars a year trying to change the way they look. But finally, the definition of what is beautiful is broadening to include ethnic diversities and all ages.

"We need to learn how to come together and be united, and to love each other with all our shades. That's one of the best things about us, all our shades and colors and hair textures. We need to love each other for all that we bring to the table and know that we're all discriminated against, we're all in the same boat. And we need to take that knowledge and go forward and fight, and not fight each other."

—Halle Berry

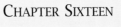

CHAPTER SIXTEEN

"Beauty Myths"

"There's something about developing strength and confidence in your physical ability that gives parameters to you. I am here. I exist. This is me. Pay attention. That, I think, is a wonderful thing for women to experience."

—Jane Fonda, actor

No matter what women accomplish, their appearances have been criteria for everything from a good marriage to success in the workplace. Women are judged, rated, and urged to measure up.

"If you look back historically, there have always been ideals of beauty. And there's nothing wrong with the cultural wish that distinguishes human beings from animals—the desire to adorn and transform the body...."

—*Naomi Wolf,*
author of The Beauty Myth

The problem starts when what we're born with is labeled unattractive.

"I hate you! I just hate you! You're ugly, fat, and stupid! Nobody likes you. Everybody else has boyfriends and girlfriends, but you've got nobody. You're just a big mess!"
—*Cathy from* Father Knows Best, *crying into a mirror*

Too fat. Too thin. Too curvy. Too flat. Throughout the twentieth century, entire industries have been created based on women's dissatisfaction with their bodies.

"The good girl mythology was no longer about chastity, it was about thinness. And so we absorbed this notion that it wasn't bad to fool around, but it was bad to 'eat around.' There was a new Puritanism about food and the body that came from our being bombarded with these images as we grew up."

—Naomi Wolf

Nowhere have women's obsessions with their bodies been more consistently focused than on the bustline—emphasized at the turn of the century, flattened for the twenties, freed in the thirties, harnessed in the fifties, liberated in the sixties, padded in the seventies, and implanted in the eighties. Breast size has been promoted as the key to happiness.

Measuring up is a rite of passage for many young women, and they often see failure with every curve.

"I learned the truth

at seventeen

that love was meant

for beauty queens."

—Janis Ian,
"Seventeen"

Left: *Actress, Jane Russell*

163

The quest for physical perfection is most publicly displayed in one of America's oldest traditions.

The Miss America Pageant began in 1921 as a publicity stunt to bring tourists to the seaside resort of Atlantic City. For decades, beauty pageant winners were sold to the public as ideal, all-American girls—perfect faces, perfect figures.

It wasn't until the late sixties that the Women's Movement began to refocus what was important. Women were working and getting degrees, but the pageant was still about parading around in bathing suits and high heels.

In 1968, six hundred women from all over the country came to Atlantic City to protest the pageant.

"We targeted the Miss America pageant as the first major over-ground demonstration of this wave of the women's movement in the United States because it summed up so many attitudes about women.

"The Miss America pageant is one institution in this country that tries to foist an image of 'femininity' and the ideal female. Well, whose ideal?—the notion of a single, plastic ideal who is of course always European, little pug nose, little blue round eyes, little golden curls, extremely thin, extremely tall, willowy, and nonchallenging, and, in a sense, nonhuman. I mean it's the Barbie image, and it isn't real any more than the Playboy centerfold, airbrushed within an inch of its pages, is real."

—Robin Morgan,
editor of Ms. *magazine*

"In my beauty pageant experience, I learned that they looked for that perfect woman—perfect hourglass figure, perfect teeth, perfect everything. And that's too much pressure to live up to. I think that the pressure to be the perfect woman is on us a lot, and I think it's very tough to understand it, then to combat it, and then to rise above it."

—Halle Berry,
actor

Beauty pageants have changed with the times; however, the notion of a single ideal of beauty still holds strong. Women still feel the pressure to be tall and beautiful.

But the conflict between what's fashionable and what's healthy has raged throughout the century. Not all women in bathing suits were in beauty contests.

Champion swimmer Annette Kellerman was one of the first to promote the idea that strong, fit bodies were beautiful at a time when women were supposed to be weak. Her book *Physical Beauty* showed that women could be healthy and attractive.

"Stoutness, plumpness, fleshiness, and obesity are only soft-pedal euphemisms. It is fat just the same. And just as clumsy, as unhealthy, as ugly, and as awkward when spelled with ten letters as with three."
—Annette Kellerman, 1918

Athletes may have felt that way, but the public didn't always agree. According to a *Photoplay* reporter of the time,

"If you want to be beautiful, don't overexercise. No woman athlete is beautiful. Here is Helen Wills, the fiend of the tennis court in action. Note the muscles on her arms, legs, and neck. Tennis did that, and Helen doesn't care. But her figure does not measure up to Hollywood standards."

Right: *Helen Wills* **Opposite page:** *Babe Didrikson, Olympic Gold Medalist and sports champion.*

Athletes like Annette Kellerman and Helen Wills redefined what was acceptable for women, but it didn't change the fact that looks still mattered.

However, for Babe Didrikson, another great sports champion, talent was more important than looks.

"Babe Didrikson was a harder sell to the public, as opposed to the current women athletes, because she was a real jock."

—Chris Evert,
athlete

The greatest woman athlete of her day was not immune to the criticism about her looks.

"Her lines and features were almost wholly masculine. A husky voice, a direct manner of speech that often drops into the sport argot, and an almost complete absence of feminine frills heighten the impression of masculinity."

—Photoplay, 1931

"I know I'm not pretty, but I try to be graceful."

—Babe Didrikson

"People came around to her, because they saw the person that she was, what was inside. She was a promoter of women's sports. I mean, she was one of the early pioneers."
—Chris Evert

Babe Didrikson's successful career in sports ended tragically at the age of forty-two. Among her major achievements were two Olympic Gold Medals, and nearly ninety major golf tournament victories.

"Sports lovers everywhere mourn the passing of Babe Didrikson, who made her name a byword with one of the most fabulous careers in sports. Her warmhearted sportsmanship never failed during her gallant, doomed, three-year fight against cancer."
—newsreel announcer Ed Herlihy, 1956

In the 1970s, Billie Jean King continued the battle for women to be accepted on athletic terms, and not to be compared to beauty queens. It was King who demanded and got equal pay for women and men at tennis's U.S. Open. It was Billie Jean King who paved the way for other women athletes like Martina Navratilova and Chris Evert, who was lionized in the early days as much for her looks as for her playing.

When Chris Evert became the youngest U.S. Open Champion, she did it wearing make-up, nail polish, and jewelry. She was "Chrissy," America's sweetheart. She was rewarded with hoards of compliments from the press.

"I'm sure, in the back of my mind, that to be a woman athlete there was still that one-percent taboo of being masculine, and I wanted to counteract that and work against it."

—Chris Evert

Top: Tennis champion, Billie Jean King. ***Bottom:*** Tennis champion, Chris Evert.

If there's an ideal of beauty for women today, it's being healthy and looking fit. Americans have experienced a workout revolution. Women have discovered that power can be beautiful.

"I think it's great that women athletes are really coming into their own and finding their stride. It's beautiful to watch. It's wonderful that there's a kind of acceptance for women as athletes, women as shining stars, competitive athletes. It's so great."
—*Jane Fonda*

"When I came up in the seventies, strong wasn't beautiful. It was looked down upon. I've seen it change. I think it's really not only accepted now, but I think young girls look up to women athletes.

Women are proud of their muscles. It means strength. It means confidence. It means beauty."

—*Chris Evert*

CHAPTER SEVENTEEN

Lucille Ball

"I think the door was opened most definitely by Lucille Ball. Lucille Ball was truly a beautiful woman, inside and out. You know, she had been a showgirl, a statuesque beauty, a serious actress, all of those things, and no one knew except Lucy, until she really started to show her wares and have her own show, what a clown she was under-neath. She showed that one could be feminine and a ragamuffin."

—Carol Burnett,
actor

*P*assionate, rebellious, imaginative, and powerful, women have, throughout the twentieth century, held a mirror up to our most cherished dreams, creating complex and fascinating visions of our lives.

But none of those visions is more persuasive than those which come into our living rooms through television.

"I'm totally a product of television. It's considered the media of women, because the demographics are all about women. I think the dirty trick that's played on us is that we are told subconsciously through television, and all forms of media really, that the more power we're told we do not have, the more we just unconsciously give up. And that's what I think television's really about."
—*Roseanne Arnold,*
actor-producer

Yet women sitting at home in their living rooms or washing dishes have, occasionally, found revolutionaries.

"There were the stereotypical women who were the moms and the aprons and the brains behind daddy going off to work, and very quiet and silent and wise and all-knowing. And, as we all know, those stereotypes, be it the men or the women, it's a crock. 'Cause it's not real life."
—*Carol Burnett*

Top: *Quintessential TV sit-com mom, Barbara Billingsley as June Cleaver.* **Bottom:** *Classic TV sit-com, "Dennis the Menace."*

LUCY: *"Who do you think does the housework?"*

ETHEL: *"And who do you think cooks all the meals?"*

RICKY: *"Oh, anybody can cook and do the housework."*

LUCY: *"Ha! I'd just like to see you two try it for a week."*

RICKY: *"OK, we will."*

FRED: *"We will?"*

LUCY: *"This I gotta see."*

—*from I Love Lucy, 1952*

"The main thing that Lucy did for me was that she acted. She was an active person who was having a grand adventure. Almost all the women I knew in my personal life and all the women on TV were passive. Once again, they were always begging the men not to go on the big adventure. And I felt like watching Lucy that she wasn't afraid of anything."

—Linda Bloodworth-Thomason,
writer-producer

"I believe in the anarchy of women. There's a lot of anarchy in her stuff and it's totally pro-female turned around, for the time that she had to do it. It's really a woman's point of view, too."

—Roseanne Arnold

In the 1950s, America celebrated suburbia. Women's magazines insisted that a man's home was his castle and women were there to serve; to get what they wanted, women were reduced to plotting and scheming. Lucy raised feminine wiles to an art form.

ETHEL: *What am I going to tell Ricky when he asks where you are?*

LUCY: *Tell him anything you want; I have nothing to hide. Tell him the truth.*

ETHEL: *Okay, I'll tell him the truth.*

LUCY: *Don't you dare!*

—*from I Love Lucy, 1956*

"The comedy and the brilliance of it, I mean, that's like at this level, but at the subtext level, this woman had to beg her husband and he didn't support her career. He's always humiliating her and spanking her. But you know what, the time that it was out, that's what she had to do."

—Roseanne Arnold

"When we look back on it now, it's silly and it's certainly very sexist. But given the time, given the way the family make-up was at that time and the male/female power ratio to one another, it was a phenomenal show."

—Linda Bloodworth-Thomason

Lucy looked like a traditional fifties housewife, but she was breaking the rules both on-screen and off. Her most radical move—having a Cuban husband.

"When I was asked to do television it was new to everyone—the networks and people in general—and the studios frowned on it. No one wanted Desi to play my husband because he was Cuban, and they wanted an 'American' couple. So we went out by ourselves in Vaudeville to prove the audiences would buy it."

—Lucille Ball on the Today show, 1983

A show about a multiethnic couple was unheard of, but audiences accepted Lucy and Ricky with open arms. And the fact that the show was so successful made it possible for Lucy to break more rules. Sex, for example: television couples slept in separate beds, and although they had children, they never seemed to have sex.

The Ricardos changed everything.

"She wasn't even allowed to say the word 'pregnant.' And then the birth of their child on television had bigger ratings than the Eisenhower swearing-in."

—Roseanne Arnold

Every week on television, Lucy was challenging the stereotypes of American wives. At the same time, Lucille Ball was breaking new ground for women in business.

Lucille Ball was the first woman to own and run her own television studio. But after her divorce from Desi Arnaz, she discovered that being the boss wasn't always easy.

"Lucy told me that when they divorced, she came in the next Monday and the script wasn't right, nothing was, and she was pretty floored. She realized then that she would have to be assertive. Before, she used to come in and do her thing, and Desi would take care of all the hiring and the firing and the rewriting of scripts and so forth, and she realized that she would have to do it now. In those days, she got a reputation for being—get this— "tough," when her husband was respected for exactly the same quality. She was feared and at times put down."
—Carol Burnett

Lucy's influence reached beyond television. She inspired generations of women not to be afraid.

"She was a phenomenal woman, because she was really imposing her personality on the world. And she was making things happen her way. She was a dreamer and a schemer, and she was going to go out there and win and get her way. And I think that was a really important message to little girls."
—Linda Bloodworth-Thomason

Two of the most successful women in television in the 1990s continue where Lucy left off—they are not afraid to make themselves heard. On *Designing Women, Evening Shade,* and other television comedies, Linda Bloodworth-Thomason has created women characters that are both feminine and feisty.

And Roseanne Arnold, as an actor and producer, brings an altogether new kind of screen heroine to television.

"I don't think there's anything degrading about being poor, or being working-class, which is another hard thing to do on television, because we're not ever supposed to talk about a class that exists in this society, and particularly a class of women. It's another invisible thing, like women of color and Jewish women and working-class women and fat women and native women and Asian women. I mean, you just never see any of that, unless they're a saint. I think that's very damaging to little girls' sense of self-esteem. And I try to do the show for the little girls out there watching."

—Roseanne Arnold

"*... I think one of the greatest tests of female strength right now, and one of the greatest challenges that we have, is to be able to take new ground and then to stand there unashamedly enjoying the view.*"

—Linda Bloodworth-Thomason

Above: *Linda Bloodworth-Thomason with "Designing Women" cast members.*

CHAPTER EIGHTEEN

"T'Ain't Nobody's Business If I Do"

"If you say the blues is a woman, it would be Bessie Smith."

—Etta James,
singer

"*A*nybody that hears a good blues song, and if you hear it by a woman, then you gonna hear the truth."
—Etta James

The blues songs of the twenties and thirties gave women a voice, and more than any other woman of her time, Bessie Smith was the blues. White women had movie stars to emulate; black women had blues singers.

"These women generally knew they were carrying not only the weight of black women in particular, but the black community on their shoulders when they went on stage."
—Daphne Duval Harrison,
historian

Bessie Smith was born in 1894 to a very poor family in Tennessee. Although she didn't have the opportunity for a formal education, she did have a voice, and she rode that voice to stardom.

"T'Ain't Nobody's Business If I Do"

There ain't nothing I can do,

or nothin' I can say,

that folks don't criticize me.

But I'm going to do

just as I want to anyway.

Unlike many of the young women who flocked to the big cities and danced at the thriving nightclubs and cabarets, Bessie Smith's success wasn't based on her looks. A promoter named Irvin C. Miller, who had a tour called "Glorifying the Brownskin Girl," considered Bessie too dark for his chorus.

"She was a natural singer, but I couldn't use her. We stressed beauty in the chorus line, and Bessie did not meet my standards as far as looks were concerned."

—*Irvin C. Miller, 1912*

She never forgot the rejection, and she never allowed it to happen to her again. Years later, at the height of her success, she stood up to Apollo Theatre Manager Frank Schiffman when he questioned whether her chorus girls were pretty enough to be on stage.

SCHIFFMAN:

"Bessie, you got a bunch of dancing girls with you this time, but they are so black, with the make-up on they'll look grey. Especially that little one at the end of the front line—she's exceptionally dark."

SMITH:

"If you don't want my girls, you don't want me. The only reason those girls look grey out there is because I don't get the proper lighting. We're coming in there, and you get me some amber lights to put on those girls. That is, if you want the show. And if you don't, I don't give a damn, because I'm tired of wearing myself out. I can go home, get drunk, and be a lady. It's up to you."

"I thought that she was one of the first feminists, even though I knew nothing about it at that time. But I always wanted to be like her. I knew that she was a no-nonsense kind of chick."

—*Etta James*

"The blues is something that you have to describe. You know, you can sing it and say the words, but it's a visual thing. It's sexual and it's humorous, and that's probably where a lot of people were intimidated, because women started to be breaking out. A woman singing—it's like she's pulling her dress up and tightening up her stockings in public. You know what I mean?"
—Etta James

As her success grew, Bessie Smith helped change the notion of what was beautiful.

"Many people do not realize that this was another function of the Blues Queens—they brought to the ordinary, workaday black women the feeling that they were beautiful, too, and not just mothers who wore themselves out, or wives or lovers who were constantly taken advantage of. They could see that here's another model for me."

—*Daphne Duval Harrison*

Bessie Smith lived hard, indulging her appetites for food, liquor, and sex with both men and women. Her music made her as rich as any movie star.

"I think Bessie Smith kinda lived according to what made her happy. And she didn't conform to what was proper or what people were expecting of a woman. She just did what Bessie Smith wanted to do."

—*Etta James*

"Nobody Knows You When You're Down and Out"

Once I lived the life of a millionaire,

Spending all my money, I didn't care.

I carried my friends out for a good time,

Buying bootleg liquor, champagne, and wine...

Bessie Smith's music reflected the turmoil in her own life. When she made her only film, *St. Louis Blues,* her husband had just walked out.

"Bessie didn't like songs unless she understood them. I don't mean the humorous songs, but the ones that came from life, they had to be about something Bessie had seen or felt. People knew that Bessie had suffered, and even after she became a star, the pain stayed in her voice, and it was real—everything about Bessie was real."

—Ruby Walker,
Bessie Smith's niece

Above: *Bessie Smith, from the movie "St. Louis Blues."*

GIRLS WIN NATIONAL A.A.U. TITLE

THE
Chicago Defender
WORLD'S ☆☆ GREATEST ☆☆☆ WEEKLY

24 PAGES
10c - Worth It

NATIONAL
EDITION

OFFICE OF PUBLICATION: 3435 INDIANA AVE. TELEPHONE CALUMET 5656

Vol. XXXIII, No. 23

THIS PAPER CONSISTS OF
TWO PARTS   PART ONE

CHICAGO, ILL., SATURDAY, OCTOBER 2, 1937

COPYRIGHT, 1937, BY ROBERT S. ABBOTT PUBLIS...

PRICE TEN CE

BESSIE SMITH, BLUES SINGER, KILLE

BROOKLYN WOMEN CHEERED IN LEGION PARADE

Story on Page 3

Mitchell Approved
Black Appointmen
Story on Page 5

MARVA FLIES TO JOE LOUIS

During the Depression, Bessie Smith's popularity declined along with the heyday of the Blues. Bessie changed her look and her act, and tried a comeback. But fate cut her career short.

On September 26, 1937, Bessie Smith was involved in a terrible car accident. She never regained consciousness.

For decades, the story persisted that Bessie Smith had died because a "Whites Only" hospital had refused to treat her.

"That kind of story probably just filtered up from the masses because the tragedy was too much for them to accept. Here was a person who was injured in a wreck, injured so terribly that she could not have survived it. And they had to do something to add to this, I imagine, because the loss was just more than they wanted to accept."

—Daphne Duval Harrison

Bessie Smith's grave was without a headstone until rock star Janis Joplin—an heiress to the Bessie Smith legacy—paid for one. Since her death, Bessie's records have sold hundreds of thousands of copies.

"I listen to her over and over again. Each time you listen to Bessie Smith, you hear new stuff. And when I listen to her, I hear every singer—each time I hear a different one—that comes after her. She picks me up, and it's like setting a crown on your head, you know, that says, 'All right, ok, so this is the way it is.'"

—Etta James

Left to right: *Aretha Franklin, Janis Joplin, and Ricki Lee Jones.*
Opposite page: *Author Alice Walker*

CHAPTER NINETEEN

Storytelling

"Literature saves us all, because it informs us all. It tells us what it is like to be human, what it is like to fall, to fail, to stumble, and somehow, miracu- lously, to rise, and to go on from darkness into darkness, still expecting to find a place that will hold all the people, all the faces, all the Adams and Eves and their countless gener- ations. That's what literature does for us."

—Maya Angelou,
author

hatever the restrictions on their lives, women always wrote. They wrote letters and diaries, plays, novels, essays, and poetry, sharing their experiences. Women writers such as Edna Ferber, Edith Wharton, Sarah Orne Jewett, Pauline Hopkins, Pearl Buck, Kate Chopin, Hilda Doolittle, Eudora Welty, Gwendolyn Brooks, and Dorothy Parker turned those experiences into literary works of enduring value.

"A woman writer will bring certain gear with her, having been born female, having been born into, maybe, a society where women are not valued very much. But a woman writer tells us that here comes somebody who has decided she's come to stay."
—Maya Angelou

Top: *Author Edith Wharton.* **Right and opposite page, top:** *Willa Cather*

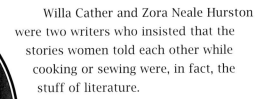

Willa Cather and Zora Neale Hurston were two writers who insisted that the stories women told each other while cooking or sewing were, in fact, the stuff of literature.

"The thing I love about Cather is that it's all tied in together—the thing of people and nature. That idea of the immigrant woman coming to settle in a place that was hard, and where life was very difficult for her. And hard work. And understanding the land became the most important part of their lives.

"When I was doing O Pioneers, when I was working on the character of Alexandra, there was one image I remember of my grandmother—a photograph. Just an old black and white photograph that must have been taken not long after she had immigrated here. This photograph of her just standing there, so innocent in a way, so pure, just looking right into the camera. It was kind of like the entire woman was revealed to you. And that's how I always felt when I read Cather's women."

—Jessica Lange,
actor

"Our neighbors were mostly Danes, Swedes, Norwegians, Bohemians. I grew fond of these immigrants—particularly the old women who used to tell me a great many stories of the old country. Their stories used to go round and round in my head at night. This was, with me, the initial response. I didn't know any writing people. I had an enthusiasm for a kind of country and a kind of people, rather than ambition...."

—Willa Cather

"Willa grew up listening to storytelling. Storytelling everywhere. In Virginia, it was the women who came down to quilt, and she would hide under the quilt frames and listen to them talk. And in Nebraska, it was the immigrant women she would visit, and they would tell her stories about their homelands. She didn't realize it at the time, but this was art. There was a kind of legacy or a bequest that was being passed among women, and also across generations of women, from mothers to daughters, from older women to younger women."

—Sharon O'Brien,
author of Willa Cather: The Emerging Voice

In her books, Cather expresses an appreciation for the work pioneer women did in building this country, but as a young girl, Cather had rebelled against any feminine expectations.

"She wanted to be a boy; she dressed in boys' clothes. She wanted to be a doctor. She wanted a role in the public world. I mean, she didn't want the domestic story of marriage and motherhood. Gender roles were so split and so divided at that time that to be public, to be powerful, you had to be masculine. You had to be male.

"Cather was a lesbian at a really complicated historical time. However, I think it would be wrong to say that she didn't write about what she most deeply cared about. So in another way, she put some of that love for women into all her characters—into mothers and daughters—and some of it went into the landscape. So, in other words, that passion ended up anyway in her fiction, even if she couldn't write about it directly."

—Sharon O'Brien

"I have no patience with love-obsessed heroines who demand more romance out of life than God put into it. These victims of over-idealization of love—they are the spoils of poets."

—Willa Cather

"She had never known before how much the country meant to her. The chirping of the insects down in the long grass had been like the sweetest music. She had felt as if her heart were hiding down there, somewhere, with the quail and the plover and the little wild things that crooned or buzzed in the sun. Under the long shaggy ridges, she felt the future stirring."

—Willa Cather,
O Pioneers!

"There was a contradiction, I suppose, between her male-identification phase and then this later celebration of women that you see in her novels. The male-identification phase was earlier, and that she moved out of when she realized the power of women's voices and the power of women's stories. And so finally, she could accept herself as a woman. Not a conventional woman, as the culture would have defined it. What she did was to take womanhood and really make it her own."

—Sharon O'Brien

For decades, Cather enjoyed great popular and critical success, including a Pulitzer Prize in 1923. Then, as the Depression plunged this country into political upheavals, her pastoral writing was dismissed as mere escapism. Today, Cather is recognized for her heroic treatment of women and her appreciation of the enduring value of the land.

"The older women having assured themselves that there were twenty kinds of cake, not counting cookies and three dozen fat pies, repaired to the corner behind the pile of watermelons, put on their white aprons and fell to their knitting and fancy work. Nils...fell into amazement at the Herculean labors those fifteen pairs of hands had performed, of the cows they had milked, the butter they had made, the gardens they had planted, the children and grandchildren they had tended, the brooms they had worn out, the amounts of food they had cooked. It made him dizzy."

—Willa Cather,
"The Bohemian Girl"

Zora Neale Hurston wrote more books than any other black female author of her time. Her writing was both intensely personal and, at the same time, representative of southern black culture of the twenties, thirties, and forties.

"No matter what others said, my mother put her trust in me. Mama exhorted her children to 'jump at de sun.' We might not land on the sun, but at least we got off the ground."

—*Zora Neale Hurston*

"There was a period when the Negro Renaissance was burgeoning in this country, and there was Zora Neale Hurston. There were men and women who were really daring to tell what it was like. Not to be white people's ideas of what it's like to be black, but what black people thought about being black."

—*Maya Angelou*

"I have tried to be as exact as possible. Keep to the exact dialect as closely as I could, having the storyteller tell it to me word for word as I wrote it down."

—*Zora Neale Hurston*

Hurston spent much of her life researching black culture—collecting folklore and recording songs.

She refused to settle down. She sought out the unusual, traveling alone throughout the country at a time when most women relied on the security of home and family.

"The strangest thing about it was once I found the use of my feet, they took to wandering. I always wanted to go. I would wander off in the woods alone, following some inside urge to go places. This alarmed my mother a great deal. She used to say she believed a woman who was an enemy of hers had sprinkled 'travel dust' around the doorstep the day I was born."
— *Zora Neale Hurston*

The seventh of eight children, Hurston was only nine years old when her mother died. In later years, she would turn this devastating experience into one of her most moving passages:

"Death finished his prowling through the house on his padded feet and entered the room. He bowed to Mama in his way and she made her manners and left us to act out our ceremonies over unimportant things. But life picked me up from the foot of Mama's bed—grief, self-despisement and all—and set my feet in strange ways. That moment was the end of a phase in my life."

In Washington, D.C., Hurston worked as a waitress to put herself through school. In New York City, she became part of a community of artists and writers who collectively embodied the Harlem Renaissance. She struck up intense friendships with writers Langston Hughes and Dorothy West. During the Depression, she obtained government grants to travel the South and record the everyday experiences of black people. Her efforts, now at the Library of Congress, kept a part of American history from being lost.

After years of artistic promise and commercial rewards, Hurston began to struggle, and her work suffered. She moved to Florida and, unable to earn a living as a writer, took odd jobs to survive. For decades, Hurston's unique voice was lost. Only now, through the efforts of writers, teachers, and literary scholars, is Hurston being rediscovered.

"Everybody means to tell the folk story. At their best, that's what writers mean to do. Miss Zora Neale Hurston is just a little sassier than many. I love her statement,

'I love myself when I am laughing.'

That's her. That's Zora Neale."
— *Maya Angelou*

"We struggled so hard to make our big

dreams come true, didn't we? The world has got-

ten some benefits from us, though we had a swell

time too. We lived! I have touched the four corners

of the horizon.... From hard searching it seems to

me that tears and laughter, love and hate, make

up the sum of life...."

—Zora Neale Hurston

CHAPTER TWENTY

Women Artists

"As a college student, I was majoring in art history and looked through the memorials that we have and found very, very few women and no principals in architecture, sculpture, painting, or music. It was pretty much women relegated to the condition of dabbler. I was taken aback that in the visual arts this was the recorded fact, except for modern dance...."

—Twyla Tharp,
*choreographer, dancer, and student
of Martha Graham*

In 1910, dancers Isadora Duncan and Ruth St. Denis shocked the world by celebrating female sensuality. They threw off their corsets, danced barefoot, and proclaimed tradition dead. Their student, Martha Graham, took that revolution and turned it into an American art form.

"Martha Graham wanted to get across the idea to everyone who would hear her that she was on fire, that to be a great dancer you had to be absolutely consumed. And if you were not, then she was not interested in you, and you were not worth the art and the art was not worth you.

"You can apply the word genius to Martha Graham; you can apply it to very few figures."

—Elizabeth Kendall,
historian

"The dancer's body is the celebrant of life. You attack dance as NOW, not what it will develop into. Not what I have done, but what I am doing."

—Martha Graham

"The body becomes a sacred garment, which is your first and your last garment, and as such it should be treated with honor and with joy and with fear, too, but always with blessing."

—Martha Graham

Above and previous page: Dancer, Ruth St. Denis.
Right and opposite page, bottom: Martha Graham dancers. *Opposite page, right:* Dancer, choreographer, and teacher Martha Graham.

By the time Graham formed the Martha Graham Dance Company in 1926, she had perfected her own style—urgent, aggressive, and abrasive, the antithesis of classical ballet.

"She said, 'Now, you're going to take off your shoes. We don't dance in ballet shoes. It's like wearing little white gloves; we don't wear little white gloves. And you're not going to have tutus, and you're not going to have toe shoes, and you're not going to have little crowns, and you're not going to have little white wings. You're going to stand there, and you're going to be like a pioneer woman standing absolutely motionless and looking out over the plains and the rivers and the mountains into the far distance....'

"There were people who found it shocking because it was not feminine. It was an all-girl group and we were not feminine, we were just dancers. We were young, American pioneer people, and she had presented it to us that way."

—Dorothy Bird,
student of Martha Graham

"You're in competition with one person only, and that is the individual you know you can become. That's the thing that makes the dancer's life the life of a realist....

"You give all your life to doing this one thing; it sounds grim, it sounds frightening, but it isn't. It has a great gaiety at times, and a great wonder."
—Martha Graham, 1957

"A woman's place in the world, for Martha Graham, was at absolute center stage. She imagined a world where a woman's psyche was the most important thing there was."
—Elizabeth Kendall

Graham was totally obsessed with her work, and she demanded nothing less from her dancers.

"Martha would never quit. With Martha it was the sense that we had to do more, that we had to do better every day, that we had to push as hard as we possibly could to accomplish as much as we possibly could."
—Twyla Tharp

"For me, it was like living in a convent, because I was so engrossed, so deeply interested, and my whole life was spent in the studio. I might as well have been in a convent. When we rehearsed at night, we would rehearse as long as Martha wanted to rehearse. And husbands would wait downstairs outside the building, and boyfriends would wait.

"I saw Erick Hawkins at the studio, and I realized that the whole thing was going to change. And of course it did. The choreography changed and the technique changed. Martha permitted him to teach ballet classes. And what had been a very private, quiet, intense working situation became tied up with many other things. The whole thing changed completely."
—Dorothy Bird

Graham and Hawkins eventually married, but he resented living in her shadow. They divorced in 1951. Graham struggled to keep her company alive, weathering financial crisis and the challenges of younger choreographers.

"She told me that she regretted terribly that she never had a child, but of course she had no time. I mean you have your regrets. But the career was the whole thing. She was a total genius."
—Dorothy Bird

"She stopped dancing at seventy-four. Her life really fell apart; she almost died. She was very ill. She picked up the pieces and went on, but it was a strange going on. The last twenty years of her life, when she wasn't dancing, she became a really big national icon."
—Elizabeth Kendall

Graham's unorthodox style lives on in the work of one of her students, choreographer and dancer Twyla Tharp.

"When I first began in 1965, for the first five years I worked only with women. We were a community because we had a common goal, because we believed in what we were doing, and because we were having an adventure. It would not have been possible for us at that time to work with men because we were non-competitive, and it had only to do with exploring the possibilities of the female body.

"Before I moved on to what was possible with male bodies, I wanted to believe that I really, really understood the female potential. Had the male element been there from the very beginning, it would have been confused. It would have been like mixed doubles in tennis—it's a very confusing sport, and I wanted to understand the solid basis before I introduced that new element."
—Twyla Tharp

"Martha was an artist who compelled and who led. She worked as a community; it was always about Martha, but it was a community of people who worked together to envision a form of theater.
—Twyla Tharp

"Some women, no matter what the era, do manage to stand up bravely and be themselves, and live a different kind of life. And they do become icons because they're such shining lights of freedom. And certainly, Martha Graham and Georgia O'Keeffe are among them."

—Gloria Steinem,
author

Independent, passionate, and strong-willed, Georgia O'Keeffe defied those who said art belonged to men.

"The men didn't want me around. They wouldn't take a woman artist seriously. I would listen to them talk and I thought, my, they are dreamy. I knew I could paint as well as some of them who were sitting around and talking.

"A woman who has lived many things and who sees lines and colors as an expression of living might say something that a man can't. I feel there is something unexplored about women that only a woman can explore. Men have done all they can do about it."

—Georgia O'Keeffe

"Georgia O'Keeffe was the first really successful American woman artist, and her success had a great deal to do both with how she looked and who she was, tough and independent."

—Benita Eisler,
historian

"I thought someone could tell me how to paint a landscape, but I never found that person. I just had to settle down and try. I thought someone could tell me how, but I found nobody could. They could tell you how they painted their landscape, but they couldn't tell me how to paint mine."

—Georgia O'Keeffe

When O'Keeffe came to New York in 1915, there was not a single major painting by an American woman hanging on a museum wall. While men determined what was art, O'Keeffe found a champion in Alfred Stieglitz.

Stieglitz was a brilliant photographer and an influential art dealer. He was also married to another woman when he became O'Keeffe's mentor, promoter, and, ultimately, lover. They defied convention by living openly with one another. It was in Stieglitz's galleries that O'Keeffe first gained recognition.

"Yesterday, O'Keeffe's exhibition opened. The show is strong: one long, loud blast of sex, sex in youth, sex in adolescence, sex in maturity, sex as gaudy as 'Ten Nights in a Whorehouse.'"
—Lewis Mumford,
art critic, 1925

"When you took time to really notice my flowers, you hung all your own associations with flowers on my flowers, and you write about my flowers as if I think and see what you think and see of the flower, and I don't."
—Georgia O'Keeffe

"On the subject of the sexual interpretation of O'Keeffe's art, I think it's fair to say that what she repudiated publicly, she encouraged or accepted privately. And she accepted it for a very important reason that makes her into the most contemporary of American artists. She knew, as she herself said, that you had to get talked about in order to have your work sell."
—Benita Eisler

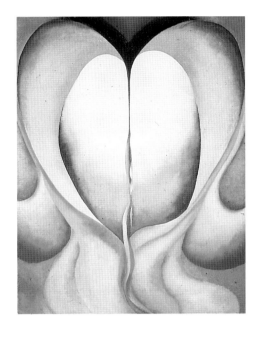

"I think O'Keeffe's paintings are profoundly erotic in the sense that life is erotic. A butterfly is erotic. A flower opening is erotic. I think that level of erotic fulfillment is in O'Keeffe's work, and our society is very hostile to that impulse."
—Judy Chicago, artist

Top: Series 1, no. 8 Opposite page: Jimson Weed

O'Keeffe was certainly talked about. First there was her love affair with Stieglitz, then there was the unabashed sexuality of her paintings, and finally there she was, nude, for all the world to see. Stieglitz had photographed her and exhibited the work in his gallery. The result was a scandal. Two years later, she opened her next exhibit to unparalleled attention.

"She, in no way, could be unaware of the fact that the following show in two years had people flocking to the gallery to see the works that were reputed to be the images, in somewhat abstract form, in painting, of the sexually liberated artist who was also a free woman, and who was living with another woman's husband, I mean, for further scandal."

—Benita Eisler

O'Keeffe and Stieglitz finally got married, but she had no use for the traditional role of wife and mother. Eventually they chose to lead separate lives. O'Keeffe visited the deserts of the Southwest and decided that landscape matched her sense of freedom and independence.

"The most important contribution of Georgia O'Keeffe to American art is that she made Modernism accessible. She told us with the early abstract pictures, and even the flower pictures— those large, blow-ups of flowers where one petal can take up the entire canvas—what that reassuring message was: that Modernism didn't have to be ugly, it didn't have to be harsh; it could be luminous colors, even luscious, Necco-wafer delicious colors, pleasing forms, and decorative."

—Benita Eisler

"I have been very fortunate, much more fortunate than most people. For instance, I can imagine myself being a much better painter and nobody paying any attention to me at all. But it happens that the thing that I have done is to have been in touch with my times, so that people have liked it. But I could have been much better and no one would have noticed. You see, a painter is one thing, and a person, in a way, is another thing. Some people seem to be luckier than others. I don't know. Maybe it's because I've taken hold of anything that came along that I wanted."

—Georgia O'Keeffe

"Such a beautiful, untouched, lonely feeling place, part of what I call The Far Away. As soon as I saw it, that was my country. I'd never seen anything like it before, but it fitted to me exactly. It's something in the air. It's just different. The sky is different. The stars are different. The wind is different."

—Georgia O'Keeffe, 1976

O'Keeffe's influences can be seen in the work of many contemporary artists, but perhaps none has been as overtly tied to the controversy over erotic content in women's work as artist Judy Chicago. The exhibition of her sculpture *The Dinner Party*, which paid homage to significant women in history, was criticized, condemned, and ultimately closed.

"I don't think I was really prepared for the amount of controversy The Dinner Party *was going to generate and continues to generate. Some of it, I think, comes from people not understanding art, and some of it comes from unfamiliarity—unfamiliarity with women's forms, with women's experiences, and with women's authentic expression.*

"The Dinner Party *was prevented from being permanently housed. What that means is: I told our story and the people who helped me also told our story, but it will only matter if our grandchildren and our great-grandchildren and their grandchildren can know that story, see that story, have that story, and be empowered by it.*

"If our relationship to history is such that the struggle to reach fulfillment over and over, and realization and achievement over and over again, is erased, then we cannot stand on the shoulders of our predecessors. And so, if O'Keeffe is not understood in the struggle for women's full creative expression, then we cannot stand on her shoulders, and young women cannot stand on mine."

—Judy Chicago,
artist

The Dinner Party

About the Historians

ELLEN CHESLER is a fellow of the Twentieth Century Fund in New York and author of *Woman of Valor: Margaret Sanger and the Birth Control Movement in America.* Dr. Chesler was an honors graduate of Vassar College and earned her master's and doctoral degrees in History from Columbia University. She is currently preparing a lecture entitled *Century of Women: Balancing Rights and Needs* for presentation at the Library of Congress in 1995.

BENITA EISLER has worked as an art editor, reporter, and on-camera corre-spondent for public television, focusing on interviews and features on the arts and culture. She has contributed articles to *The New Yorker, Vanity Fair,* and *Mirabella,* and has written books which include *The Lowell Offering: Writings by New England Mill Women: 1840-1845; Class Act: A Study of Social Mobility in America; Private Lives: Men and Women of the 50's;* and the dual biography *O'Keeffe and Stieglitz: An American Romance.* She was educated at Smith and Harvard and has taught the 19th and 20th century novel at Princeton.

ESTELLE FREEDMAN received her M.A. and Ph.D. in history from Columbia University. She is the author of several books, including *Intimate Matters: A History of Sexuality in America* and *Their Sisters' Keepers: Women's Prison Reform in America,* as well as numerous articles dealing with women's history. Dr. Freedman is currently on the faculty of Stanford University, where she is writing a biography of American prison reformer Miriam Van Waters.

PAULA GIDDINGS is the author of two books on the social and political histo-ry of African-American women: *When and Where I Enter: The Impact of Black Women on Race and Sex in America* and *In Search of Sisterhood: Delta Sigma Theta and the Challenge of the Black Sorority Movement.* She has written extensively on international and national issues and has been a book editor for Howard University Press, acquiring important texts on African-American history and literature. In 1990, she was awarded an Honorary Doctorate of Humane Lettres from Bennett College. In 1993, Dr. Giddings was named a Fellow of the National Humanities Center and the John Simon Guggenheim Foundation. She is currently writing a biography of Ida B. Wells.

ALICE KESSLER HARRIS is the author of several books, including *Out to Work: A History of Wage-Earning Women in the United States; Women Have Always Worked: A Historical Overview;* and *A Woman's Wage: Historical Meanings and Social Consequences.* She has written numerous articles on issues relating to women's history, work and workers, and contemporary social policy. Dr. Kessler Harris graduated from Goucher College and received her M.A. and Ph.D. in History from Rutgers University. She has taught at Hoffstra University, and Temple University and is currently

Director of the Women's Studies Program and Professor of History at Rutgers University.

DAPHNE HARRISON is a noted authority on African-American music, having published a number of books and articles on blues and jazz, specifically black women in blues. Dr. Harrison received her master's degree in Music from Northwestern University, and her PhD in Education from the University of Miami, Florida. In 1992, she was awarded an NEH Fellowship for research on black women in the African American Musical Theatre, 1900-1940.

ELIZABETH KENDALL, a noted historian, dance critic, and journalist, has published extensively on dance in America and Russia, including *Where She Danced* and "Home to Russia: Dance Theater of Harlem in the USSR." Consultant for the WNET history of world dance and for the Ford Foundation Office of the Arts, she is also a dance critic for *Harper's Bazaar.*

VALERIE MATSUMOTO is Associate Professor of History and Asian American Studies at UCLA. She is author of *Farming the Home Place: A Japanese American Community in California, 1919-1982* and is currently working on a book about Nisei women writers in the 1930s. Dr. Matsumoto received her M.A. and her Ph.D. in U.S. History from Stanford University.

SHARON O'BRIEN is Professor of English and American Studies at Dickinson College, where she has taught since 1975. She received her Ph.D. in English and American Literature from Harvard University and has written a large volume of material on American author Willa Cather, including *Willa Cather: The Emerging Voice,* and has edited *The Library of America Willa Cather, Vol. I and II.*

VICKI RUIZ is the Andrew W. Mellon All-Clairmont Professor in the Humanities and Chair, Department of History, at Clairmont graduate school. She received her Ph.D. in history from Stanford University. She is the co-editor with Ellen DuBois of *Unequal Sisters: A Multi-Cultural Reader in U.S. Women's History, 1st and 2nd editions,* and author of *Cannery Women, Cannery Lives: Mexican Women, Unionization, and the California Food Processing Industry, 1930-1950.* Dr. Ruiz is currently working on a history of Mexican women in the United States.

SUSAN WARE has served since 1988 on the Advisory Board of the Arthur and Elizabeth Schlesinger Library on the History of Women in America. She obtained her PhD from Harvard University, with a special interest in the history of American women, and has published several books, including *Beyond Suffrage: Women in the New Deal* and *Still Missing: Amelia Earhart and the Search for Modern Feminism.* Dr. Ware is currently Associate Professor, Department of History, New York University.

$\mathscr{P}$hotographic Sources

The Walker Collection of A'Lelia Perry Bundles
Madam C. J. Walker Collection, Indiana Historical Society
Academy of Motion Picture Arts and Sciences
Carl Van Vechten
Chris Albertson
The Chicago Defender
Universal City Studios, Inc. Courtesy of MCA Publishing Rights, a Division of MCA Inc.
Fannie Lou Hamer Papers, The Amistad Research Center, Tulane University, New Orleans
Associated Press
AP/Wide World Photos
Archive Photos
The Georgia O'Keeffe Foundation/Artists Rights Society (ARS), New York
Arnold Newman
Bettye Lane
Brown Brothers
McClung Historical Collection, Knox County Public Library System
Chicago Sun-Times
Cirrincione Lee Entertainment
Elizabeth Arden
Jane Fonda and A*VISION Entertainment
Cleveland Public Library Photograph Collection
JoCarol Nesset-Sale
Cleveland Plain Dealer
The Roosevelt Library
George Meany Memorial Archives
Collection of the J. Paul Getty Museum, Malibu, California
ILGWU Archives, Labor-Management, Documentation Center, Cornell Universiy
Harry Richards Film Collection, Estuary Press, Oakland, California
The Huntington Library, San Marino, California
Immigrant City Archives, Lawrence, MA
Delilah Jackson Collection, Black Patti Research
Collection of Akiko Matsui, Japanese American National Museum
Japanese American Historical Archives
The John F. Kennedy Library
Library of Congress
Los Angeles Times
The McCardell Family Collection
The Archives and Special Collections on Women in Medicine, Medical College
    of Pennsylvania
Gene Arias
National Archives
The National PTA
Nebraska State Historical Society
The New-York Historical Society
Photographs and Prints Division, Schomberg Center for Research in Black Culture,
    The New York Public Library, Astor, Lenox and Tilden Foundations
Henry W. and Albert A. Berg Collection, The New York Public Library, Astor, Lenox
    and Tilden Foundations
United States History, Local History & Genealogy Division, The New York Public Library,
    Astor, Lenox and Tilden Foundations
The Dorothea Lange Collection, The Oakland Museum, Gift of Paul S. Taylor
Frank and Marie-Therese Wood Print Collections
Planned Parenthood® Federation of America, Inc.
Ralph W. Miller Golf Library/Museum
Alexander C. Sanger
Purdue University and the Purdue Research Foundation
Phyllis Schlafly
Revlon
Schlesinger Library, Radcliffe College
Schlesinger Library, Radcliffe College Archives
Woman's Party Corporation, Sewall-Belmont House
Division of Costume, The National Museum of American History, Smithsonian Institution
The National Air and Space Museum, Smithsonian Institution
Sophia Smith Collection, Smith College
Southern University
Collection of the United States Supreme Court
Caresse Crosby Collection, Morris Library, Southern Illinois University
Miss America Organization
The Stanford University Archives

Tina Hill
Judy Chicago, Through the Flower
Donald Woodman
University Research Library, University of California, Los Angeles
Davidson Library, University of California, Santa Barbara
Joseph J. Pennell Collection, Kansas Collection, University of Kansas Libraries
The New York Times Company
NYT Pictures
Vermont Historical Society
Beinecke Rare Book and Manuscript Library, Yale University
Special Collections, Vassar College Libraries
Archives of Labor and Urban Affairs, Wayne State University
Sarah Weddington
Winston-Salem Journal
Women's Bureau, U.S. Dept. of Labor
State Historical Society of Wisconsin
Jean Weisinger

PHOTO CREDITS

JACKET

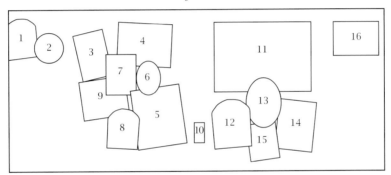

1. Library of Congress
2. Courtesy of *Consolidated News/* Archive Photos
3. Courtesy of National Archives
4. New York Public Library
5. Library of Congress
6. Photographic Collection/Los Angeles Public Library
7. Courtesy of Arnold J. Saxe/Archive Photos
8. Library of Congress

9. Japanese American Historical Archive
10. Nebraska State Historical Society
11. Photographic Collection/Los Angeles Public Library
12. Courtesy of Archive Photos
13. Courtesy of Delilah Jackson Collection
14. Schlesinger Library, Radcliffe College
15. Collection of the U.S. Supreme Court
16. Library of Congress

PART ONE

p. 4-5, Courtesy of The Huntington Library, San Marino, California
p. 6-7, Collection of the New-York Historical Society
p. 8, top left, Library of Congress
p. 8, bottom, Courtesy of American Stock/Archive Photos
p. 9, top, Courtesy of National Archives
p. 9, bottom, ILGWU Archives, Labor-Management, Documentation Center, Cornell University
p. 10, top, Schlesinger Library, Radcliffe College
p. 10, bottom inset, ILGWU Archives, Labor-Management, Documentation Center, Cornell University
p. 10, bottom, Brown Brothers
p. 11, top, ILGWU Archives, Labor-Management, Documentation Center, Cornell University

p. 11, bottom, Courtesy of George/Archive Photos
p. 12-13, Library of Congress
p. 13, center, Courtesy of Archive Photos
p. 14, center, Library of Congress
p. 14, bottom left, Schlesinger Library, Radcliffe College
p. 14, bottom center, ILGWU Archives, Labor-Management, Documentation Center, Cornell University
p. 14, bottom right, Schlesinger Library, Radcliffe College
p. 15, center, Library of Congress
p. 15, top right, Library of Congress
p. 16, top, Collection of Immigrant City Archives, Lawrence, MA
p. 16, bottom, Library of Congress
p. 17, top, Library of Congress
p. 17, bottom, Collection of Immigrant City Archives, Lawrence, MA
p. 18, top, Collection of Immigrant City Archives, Lawrence, MA
p. 18, center, Brown Brothers
p. 19, top, Courtesy of Archive Photos
p. 19, bottom, Schlesinger Library, Radcliffe College
p. 20, top, Schlesinger Library, Radcliffe College
p. 20, bottom, Schlesinger Library, Radcliffe College Archives
p. 21, top left, Courtesy of the National PTA
p. 21, bottom right, Courtesy of the National PTA
p. 22, Schlesinger Library, Radcliffe College
p. 23, top, Schlesinger Library, Radcliffe College
p. 23, bottom, Schlesinger Library, Radcliffe College
p. 24, Alice Perham, photographer. Courtesy Vermont Historical Society
p. 25, top left, Schlesinger Library, Radcliffe College
p. 25, bottom left, Schlesinger Library, Radcliffe College
p. 25, top right, Collection of Immigrant City Archives, Lawrence, MA
p. 26, Schlesinger Library, Radcliffe College
p. 27, top, Schlesinger Library, Radcliffe College
p. 27, bottom, Schlesinger Library, Radcliffe College
p. 28, Courtesy of Lass/Archive Photos
p. 29, Library of Congress
p. 30, top, United States History, Local History & Genealogy Division, The New York Public Library, Astor, Lenox and Tilden Foundations
p. 30, bottom, Library of Congress
p. 31, top, George Meany Memorial Archives
p. 31, bottom, Women's Bureau, U.S. Dept. of Labor
p. 32, Photographs and Prints Division, Schomburg Center for Research in Black Culture, The New York Public Library, Astor, Lenox and Tilden Foundations
p. 33, Courtesy Robert Trinkle
p. 34, top, Courtesy of Archive Photos
p. 34, center, Courtesy National Archives
p. 34, right, Photographs and Prints Division, Schomburg Center for Research in Black Culture, The New York Public Library, Astor, Lenox and Tilden Foundations
p. 35, top right, Courtesy Tina Hill
p. 35, bottom, George Meany Memorial Archives
p. 36, top, Library of Congress
p. 36, center, Library of Congress
p. 36, bottom, Department of Special Collections, University Reserach Library, University of California, Los Angeles
p. 37, top, Library of Congress
p. 37, bottom, Library of Congress
p. 38, Courtesy National Archives
p. 39, Courtesy National Archives
p. 40, top, Courtesy of Anthony Statile/Archive Photos
p, 40, bottom, Courtesy of Camerique/Archive Photos
p. 41, top, Courtesy of Lambert/Archive Photos
p. 41, bottom, Courtesy of Lambert/Archive Photos
p. 42, Courtesy of Lambert/Archive Photos
p. 43, top right, Courtesy of Jay Florian Mitchell/Archive Photos
p. 43, bottom left, Courtesy of Ewing Krainin/Archive Photos
p. 44, top, Courtesy of Camerique/Archive Photos
p. 44, bottom, Courtesy of Gerald Davis/Archive Photos
p. 45, top, Courtesy National Archives
p. 45, bottom, Harry Richards Film Collection, Estuary Press, Oakland, CA
p. 46, top left, Archives of Labor and Urban Affairs, Wayne State University
p. 46, right, Harry Richards Film Collection, Estuary Press, Oakland, CA
p. 47, top, Archives of Labor and Urban Affairs, Wayne State University
p. 47, bottom, Archives of Labor and Urban Affairs, Wayne State University
p. 48, top, Archives of Labor and Urban Affairs, Wayne State University
p. 48, bottom, Archives of Labor and Urban Affairs, Wayne State University
p. 49, Courtesy Aileen Hernandez
p. 50, top, Courtesy of the John F. Kennedy Library
p. 50, bottom, Photographs ©Bettye Lane
p. 51, top, Courtesy of Ruth Bader Ginsburg
p. 51, bottom, Courtesy of Consolidated News Pictures-Ron Sachs/Archive Photos

p. 53, Reprinted with permission of Associated Press/WideWorld Photos
p. 54, Courtesy of JoCarol Nesset-Sale. Reprinted with permission of *Cleveland Plain Dealer*
p. 55, top, Courtesy of JoCarol Nesset-Sale. Reprinted with permission of the *Lakewood Sun-Times.*
p. 55, bottom, Reprinted with permission of the *Lakewood Sun-Times.*
p. 56, Library of Congress
p. 57, top left, Courtesy of Phyllis Schlafly
p. 57, top right, Reprinted with permission of Associated Press/Wide World Photos
p. 57, bottom, Reprinted with permission of Associated Press/Wide World Photos
p. 59, Library of Congress
p. 60, top left, Courtesy of Archive Photos
p. 60, center, Courtesy of American Stock/Archive Photos
p. 60, bottom left, Courtesy of Agence France Presse/Archive Photos
p. 60, bottom right, Courtesy of Archive Photos
p. 61, Collection of Immigrant City Archives, Lawrence, MA

PART TWO

p. 64-65, Library of Congress
p. 66-67, Henry W. and Albert A. Berg Collection, The New York Public Library, Astor, Lenox and Tilden Foundations
p. 68, center, Courtesy of Archive Photos
p. 68, bottom, Schelsinger Library, Radcliffe College
p. 69, top, Courtesy of Archive Photos
p. 69, right, Library of Congress
p. 70, left, Courtesy of Albert Rose/Archive Photos
p. 70, right, Library of Congress
p. 71, top, The Stanford University Archives
p. 71, bottom, The Stanford University Archives
p. 72, left, The Stanford University Archives
p. 72-73, background, The Stanford University Archives
p. 73, right, The Stanford University Archives
p. 74, top left, Courtesy National Archives
p. 74, bottom left, Courtesy of American Stock/Archive Photos
p. 74, bottom right, Courtesy of American Stock/Archive Photos
p. 75, Henry W. and Albert A. Berg Collection, The New York Public Library, Astor, Lenox and Tilden Foundations
p. 76, top, Courtesy of Special Collections, Vassar College Libraries
p. 76, center, Courtesy of Special Collections, Vassar College Libraries
p 76, bottom, Courtesy of Special Collections, Vassar College Libraries
p. 77, top right, Henry W. and Albert A. Berg Collection, The New York Public Library, Astor, Lenox and Tilden Foundations
p. 77, center, Courtesy of Special Collections, Vassar College Libraries
p. 78, top left, Schlesinger Library, Radcliffe College
p. 78, center, Courtesy of Alexander C. Sanger
p. 79, Courtesy of Alexander C. Sanger
p. 80, top left, Courtesy of Alexander C. Sanger
p. 80-81, Library of Congress
p. 81, top right, Planned Parenthood® Federation of America, Inc.
p. 82, top left, Schlesinger Library, Radcliffe College
p. 82, bottom, Courtesy of Cleveland Public Library Photograph Collection
p. 83, Joseph J. Pennell Collection, Kansas Collection, University of Kansas Libraries
p. 84, Sophia Smith Collection, Smith College
p. 85, top right, Sophia Smith Collection, Smith College
p. 85, center, Sophia Smith Collection, Smith College
p. 86, top left, Sophia Smith Collection, Smith College
p. 86, center, Library of Congress
p. 86-87, Copyright ©1915 by The New York Times Company. Reprinted by permission.
p. 87, right, Sophia Smith Collection, Smith College
p. 88, top, Planned Parenthood® Federation of America, Inc.
p. 88, bottom, Courtesy of Alexander C. Sanger
p. 89, top, Courtesy of Alexander C. Sanger
p. 89, bottom, Courtesy of Alexander C. Sanger
p. 90, Planned Parenthood® Federation of America, Inc.
p. 91, Courtesy of Alexander C. Sanger
p. 92, Reprinted with permission of Associated Press/Wide World Photos
p. 93, Courtesy of Archive Photos
p. 94, Courtesy of Lambert/Archive Photos
p. 95, top, Courtesy of Tucker Ranson/Archive Photos
p. 95, bottom, Courtesy of Popperfoto/Archive Photos
p. 96, photograph ©Jim Marshall
p. 97, top left, Courtesy of Express Newspapers/Archive Photos

p. 97, top right, Courtesy of Lambert/Archive Photos

p. 97, bottom right, Frank and Marie-Therese Wood Print Collection, Alexandria, VA

p. 98, Courtesy of Archive Photos

p. 99, Courtesy of Douglas Corry/Archive Photos

p. 101, Courtesy of Archive Photos

p. 102, top, Library of Congress

p. 102, bottom, Library of Congress

p. 103, Schlesinger Library, Radcliffe College

p. 104, Photographs and Prints Division, Schomberg Center for Research in Black Culture, The New York Public Library, Astor, Lenox and Tilden Foundations

p. 105, top, Frank and Marie-Therese Wood Print Collection, Alexandria, VA

p. 105, bottom, Library of Congress

p. 106, left, ©1917. Reprinted with permission of the Los Angeles Times

p. 106, right, Woman's Party Corporation, Sewall-Belmont House, Washington, D.C.

p. 107, top, Woman's Party Corporation, Sewall-Belmont House, Washington, D.C.

p. 107, bottom, Schlesinger Library, Radcliffe College.

p. 108, top left, Woman's Party Corporation, Sewall-Belmont House, Washington, DC

p. 108, center, Harry T. Burn Collection, McClung Historical Collection, Knox County Public Library System, Knoxville, Tennessee

p. 108, bottom left, Harry T. Burn Collection, McClung Historical Collection, Knox County Public Library System, Knoxville, Tennessee

p. 109, Library of Congress

p. 110, Library of Congress

p. 111, Courtesy of Archive Photos

p. 112, The Dorothea Lange Collection, The Oakland Museum, Gift of Paul S. Taylor

p. 113, top, Courtesy of Archive Photos

p. 113, bottom, Courtesy of American Stock/Archive Photos

p. 113, inset, Library of Congress

p. 114, top, Courtesy of the Roosevelt Library

p. 114, bottom, Courtesy of the Roosevelt Library

p. 115, top, Courtesy of Archive Photos

p. 115, center, Courtesy of the Roosevelt Library

p. 115, bottom, Courtesy of Popperfoto/Archive Photos

p. 116, top, ©Associated Press/Wide World Photos. Courtesy of the Roosevelt Library

p. 116, bottom, Women's Bureau, U.S. Dept. of Labor

p. 117, top, Courtesy of the Roosevelt Library

p. 117, bottom, ©1994 *Chicago Sun-Times.* Reprinted with permission

p. 118, top, Library of Congress

p. 118, bottom, Library of Congress

p. 119, top right, Photographs and Prints Division, Schomberg Center for Research in Black Culture, The New York Public Library, Astor, Lenox and Tilden Foundations

p. 119, bottom, Courtesy of Archive Photos

p. 120, Courtesy of Popperfoto/Archive Photos

p. 121, Library of Congress

p. 122, Fannie Lou Hamer Papers, The Amistad Research Center, Tulane University, New Orleans, Louisiana

p. 123, top, Courtesy of Express Newspapers/Archive Photos

p. 123, center, Courtesy of Arnold Sachs/Archive Photos

p. 123, bottom, Courtesy of Archive Photos

p. 124, George Meany Memorial Archives

p. 125, Courtesy of Archive Photos

p. 126, top, Courtesy of State Historical Society of Wisconsin

p. 126, bottom, Courtesy of National Archives

p. 127, Courtesy of Archive Photos

p. 128, Fannie Lou Hamer Papers, The Amistad Research Center, Tulane University, New Orleans, Louisiana

p. 129, center, Frank and Marie-Therese Wood Print Collections, Alexandria, VA

p. 129, bottom, Fannie Lou Hamer Papers, The Amistad Research Center, Tulane University, New Orleans, Louisiana

p. 131, Photographs ©Bettye Lane

p. 132, top, Photographs ©Bettye Lane

p. 132, bottom, Photographs ©Bettye Lane

p. 133, Photographs ©Bettye Lane

p. 134, Photographs ©Bettye Lane

p. 135, Courtesy of Sarah Weddington

p. 136, Photographs ©Bettye Lane

p. 137, top, Reprinted with permission of the *Winston-Salem Journal*

p. 137, bottom, Photographs ©Bettye Lane

p. 138, Copyright ©The New York Times Company. Reprinted by permission.

p. 139, top, Courtesy of Jim Wells/Archive Photos

p. 139, bottom, ©1993 Reprinted with permission of the *Los Angeles Times.* Photograph reprinted with permission of Associated Press/Wide World Photos

COLOPHON

*This book was edited, designed and produced by Executive Edition under
the art direction and production management of Candace J. Magee.*

Editor: Alan Covey
Design: Laurie Shock
Production Coordinator: Kim Knox Norman
Photographic Permissions: Beth Lilly (Turner Photo Services)
Editorial Assistants: Martha Basile and Vicky Holifield